A Memoir of Loss & Resilience

MOLDed

CAROL MILBERGER, Ph.D.

Paperback - ISBN: 979-8-9907401-1-2
EBook - ISBN: 979-8-9907401-0-5

Design by Vanessa Mendozzi
Printed in the United States of America

Dedicated to Wayne, the master fixer.

CONTENTS

FRIDAY NIGHT RAIN

When Tropical Storm Fay let loose on the Texas coastal plains in early September of 2002, it appeared she planned to stay. Houston's Channel 13 predicted heavy rain, flash floods, and strong wind gusts. I was grateful we only had torrential rains and glad we were all home safe for the evening.

My husband, Wayne, sipped Dr Pepper, his only vice. No one could believe he was fifty-five, he didn't look over forty. He was strong and vibrant, with sandy brown hair and an almost-constant smile. We lived in a beautiful home on four lush acres in a small town sixty miles outside Houston. Mostly unheard of, like most small towns, Harrison was a wonderful place to raise a family. I remember glancing up from the stove to see our barefoot kids blissfully cartwheeling on the plush grass, swinging till toes touched cotton ball clouds, or zipping down the long slide.

Life was balanced, or as balanced as possible with two careers and three active children. Our family was healthy, happy, and busy, and my life operated at a steady trot with time allowed for relaxing stops along the way.

A junior in high school, Christine was ecstatic to spend a rare Friday night at home, which added excitement to the dinner table as lightning blasted across the backyard sky. Between games and practice for cheerleading, band, volleyball, debate, and more, Christine was glad for an evening to recover. She was petite, only 5' 2", a trait inherited from her dad's side; but the blue eyes and almond hair came from both of us. Christine was sweet, thoughtful, responsible, and an overachiever of biblical proportions.

Christine flashed an orthodontist-approved smile as she grabbed a slice of pizza. "I'm glad the football game was cancelled. It would be awful cheering in this rain!"

I beamed. "You need a night off. I'm glad everyone is home safe tonight."

We watched the lightning flash. Wayne and twelve-year-old Shelby slowly counted in unison: "One one thousand, two one thousand, three one thousand," then stopped as deep thunder took over. Wayne announced how many miles we were from the storm's center.

My "glad to be home safe" comment led to an expected reaction from Shelby, who lived to be with friends and wasn't happy stuck at home with family. Shelby noticed early that perfection was taken by her older sister, so she settled for being Shelby. She shared coloring and stature with her sister, but the Texas-size spirit belonged only to Shelby. Shelby was bright, quick, fearless, and extremely social.

Right on cue, Shelby asked, "Can Madison come over?" We heard this so frequently, Wayne used it as her middle name, as in, "Here comes Shelby 'Can-Madison-come-over' Milberger."

"No, honey. This is a big storm. There might even be flooding," I replied.

Unfazed, she continued, "But she lives just down the street."

"No, Shelby, not tonight. No one is coming or going; we're all staying home."

"But her parents don't care." She was determined, and just warming up.

"Shelby!" I responded sharply. We'd done this dance many times.

"Okay; so, like, maybe tomorrow?"

"Sure. Maybe tomorrow."

She grinned down at her plate.

Our quiet, thoughtful eleven-year-old, Justin, slid a slice of pizza from the box. He glanced up with clear saucer-sized eyes, "So, Mom, will I have to be in all those activities like Christine when I'm in high school?"

I stammered, then said it wasn't required to be in every high school club, sport, and activity, like his big sister.

"Good!" he replied with more energy than I expected. I added disclaimers about how fun it was to be active and engaged, but he didn't respond. Christine chimed in to say she loved being busy, but Justin was finished with the pizza and the conversation. He reached for his crutches, then hopped up from the antique oak table. He had broken his leg in gym class a few weeks earlier and would spend six weeks in a full cast. While Justin arranged crutches under each arm, Wayne asked if he needed anything.

"Cancel homework for all of sixth grade?" Justin grinned, then gracefully swung across the kitchen tile. Justin had a dry sense of humor, and was bright, kind, and quiet. He wasn't interested in following either sister, and wasn't an overachiever or a fearless extrovert. A couple of friends, free time to kick back, a great book, and he was happy. His Pokémon phase was over, but he still enjoyed watching Homer Simpson grouse on TV.

Shelby put her plate in the sink, then followed Justin to the den. Shelby was starting seventh grade, and Justin was in sixth. While they were twenty months apart in age, Justin's late summer birthdate put him only one grade behind Shelby.

Shelby was proving to be a handful, and we struggled to keep her in check. Last year she was sent home from a church dance for inappropriate behavior, then tried to sneak out after midnight a few months later. She didn't sneak out in the traditional sense. She warned she might leave after we fell asleep since she couldn't get permission to go where she wanted. She was eleven, so from my perspective there was no place she could go after midnight. That episode ended well because we intercepted her farewell note, and her, before she implemented her amazingly flawed plan. The interception occurred because I lay in a frozen-awake state until her note silently swished under our bedroom door. Not sleeping wasn't a sustainable strategy for me, so clearly the teen years wouldn't be easy.

As I contemplated age thirteen, I felt I was playing chess for her soul. She'd make a move, I'd block her, and then we'd repeat. We did more than play imagined chess for her life. She saw a counselor, and Wayne and I had joined her for family sessions the year before. By all accounts we were doing a good job, but good parenting didn't guarantee safe children, especially during the teen years. Shelby was terribly bored in school, but there were few alternatives in our small town.

Christine rinsed her plate, then joined her siblings in the den for a rare evening at home. Looking back, I should have hugged her again and told her to slow down. I did so, many times, but she was determined to overachieve, then secure a slot in an excellent university. She loved being involved in virtually every activity, something that was only possible in a small high school. She didn't rest during the football halftime show, but dashed back on the field in her cheerleading uniform to perform with the marching band. She remained double-booked, Hermione-style, all through high school.

Wayne and I gazed at the towering pecan trees slowly swaying in the driving rain. I noticed water pooling in the field behind the house, then asked if it would reach us. I was, and still am, a world-class worrier. I could teach worrying at the graduate level.

Wayne smiled, "No. We're in the five-hundred-year flood plain, so that's really unlikely."

Wanting a distraction from the storm's incessant rain and potential flooding, I asked Wayne what he liked best about our remodeling project. To adjust to our family's changing needs, we'd transformed the three-car garage into a den, laundry room, bathroom, and Christine's bedroom.

"What do I like best? Easy; I like the fact that it's over." He came from a long line of teasers; it must be genetic for a trait to be that strong.

"No. I'm serious."

"So am I." Maybe he felt sorry for me, because he relented. "I like the additional bedroom and bathroom for Christine. Adding the den makes it more livable." His smile lines deepened. "You probably enjoy the large laundry room, right?" He waited for me to react to the laundry comment, but I was too preoccupied. He leaned back in the steel-gray leather recliner, "I guess I like the big detached garage most. I like having my tools in one location, and a place to work when the weather's bad."

Wayne was a mechanical engineer turned turf-grass farmer and rancher who focused our investments into farm and ranch purchases because land was something "they couldn't make more of." Maintaining tools, tractors, and other farm equipment was a core value, and having space to work was important to him.

"If you could take anything in a fire, what furniture would you take?" I was so happy with our life I wanted to extend the conversation.

"You know I'd take my desk and chair." Wayne loved his gigantic antique oak desk and matching "king" chair with ornate arms and legs.

"I'd take my bookcase." Elaborate carved doors graced the front of my handsome antique oak bookcase. I could have selected the pedestal kitchen table or the leaded-glass china cabinet beside it. We were surrounded by items I loved, eclectic pieces that brought beauty, interest, and comfort to our home. Countless afternoons spent tipping BBQ-scented auction paddles under canvas tents while our children played in the dirt near our folding metal chairs had paid off.

My gaze lingered on the oak Windsor rocking chair next to a large potted fern; my reading spot would be ready when I had time in a few years. Behind the chair was a huge gray river-rock fireplace with a sandstone ledge and large windows flanking both sides. As toddlers, the kids spent hours vrooming Matchbox cars and skirting talkative Little People along that ledge, occasionally stopping to peer at a kitty cat, squirrel, or daddy in the yard.

As I watched the rain outside the kitchen window, I remembered how booming thunderstorms prompted the kids to play "hurricane" when they were little. They draped quilts over the couch and confiscated kitchen chairs, then scattered through the house gathering pillows, quilts, and a pink plastic tea set. Christine directed the action and held the primary speaking role. As toddlers, Shelby and Justin performed age-appropriate parts. Once the tent was stocked, Christine peered past the quilt-covered doorway until she spotted Justin dutifully tottering back and forth across the tile. Christine declared in a concerned adult voice, "Oh, no! There's a little lost boy outside!"

They'd coax the lonely child inside with pretzels while Christine continued her reassuring banter: "Don't worry, Honey, we'll find your mommy and daddy soon. But you can stay with us until the storm is over."

The lost child was always pre-verbal, or in shock, because he would simply nod or shake his head in response to questions. This exchange was relayed loudly for the rest of the world, "He *is* lost but he *does* have a mommy and daddy!" Over time, they'd switch roles, but the lost child never had a speaking part, just emphatic head movements and serious eye contact. Silent movies had nothing on this troupe.

The game went on for hours, with necessary breaks to retrieve a stuffed animal or other creature comfort. They ducked out of the tent with a hurried, "Be right back!" to dart through the pretend rainstorm. They played with a vengeance.

Their squeals of delight sounded sweeter and more precious against the pounding rain. Watching their joyful production fill those lazy, long afternoons while the wind buffeted towering trees nourished me at a deep level. Of course our children valued their shelter most when it was at risk. Terrifying lightning flashes and thunder whose intensity overtook all other sounds confirmed the fragility, and importance, of shelter. Remaining safe and dry inside their tent, inside our house, was so vital they enshrined it through play.

That evening, Wayne and I settled in the living room to watch *A Beautiful Mind* while the kids watched a movie in the den. It was wonderful spreading out to two living areas now that remodeling was over.

Around 4:30 a.m. I padded to the kitchen for the fourth time to check the backyard. Regular checks didn't stop the rain and pooling water, but I was undeterred since conscientiousness paid off handsomely in many aspects of my life. I flipped on the outdoor lights to peer through the window. Wayne's slippers trod softly on the tile, then soundlessly across the living room area rug.

He leaned over my shoulder. "Is it still there?"

I turned to him. "Now it has waves!"

"Never thought this property would be lakefront," he chuckled.

"This is serious," I chided. "We have a lake lapping in the backyard and the rain is relentless!"

Wayne waited for the deep thunder to subside. "Don't worry. That low spot is over twenty yards away. The water won't get to the house."

Part of Wayne's turf grass skill set included determining and modifying how water drains across land, as well as understanding how land holds water. When he pointed out a low spot and said we didn't need to worry, that carried the weight of the conversation.

Since neither of us could sleep, we decided to dress, then drive through the neighborhood to check other low-lying areas. I stepped into the thick damp air under the shelter of the porte-cochere while rain plummeted in solid sheets on either side. I'd taken showers with less water pressure!

Wayne hopped in the truck and pushed the garage door remote. "I checked the rain gauge. We got nineteen inches since yesterday; this is a really big rain!"

Excited to be on a pre-sunrise adventure together, I chattered as we crept along the dark road. A neighbor's driveway disappeared under a small lake spanning the yards of several homes. Wayne rotated the truck so the headlights illuminated the water-covered driveway, then leaned over the steering wheel to say they'd be stuck home for a while. Again, I asked if he thought the water would reach our house. He reassured me that it wouldn't; that everything would be okay.

The beating rain, deep rumbling thunder, and frantic windshield wipers filled in the blanks as we drove to town. I stared at the drainage ditch brimming with water.

Wayne glanced over while stopped at a red light, "I forgot to tell you, the bathroom floor had water on it last night."

I shifted uncomfortably. "We've never had water come in. Where did it come from?"

"Don't know. It was on the floor between the shower and bathtub. It was less than one cup of water, so don't worry. It will be fine."

Once we returned home, I checked our bathroom to make sure the floor was still dry. I watched the rain pound the ferns and bushes outside the huge windows flanking the bathtub. We'd had plenty of rainstorms, but never a leak. One cup of water on a tile floor really wasn't cause for alarm, at least at that time.

By late morning the rain finally stopped and the sun burst out with a vengeance well known to the Texas Gulf coast. The steam bath resumed; it hit 94 degrees with 87 percent humidity later that day. I said a brief prayer of gratitude that the storm was over and our house was undamaged.

Wayne rushed in the back door after checking the garden, declaring, "Man, it's hotter than a two-dollar pistol out there!" He was a native Texan, and his slow drawl gave him away quickly. In fact, it drew initial shock, then smiles, when he was introduced to my East Coast brothers. I admit during my first years in Houston I assumed people who talked slow also thought slow, if thinking occurred at all. I soon learned that not sounding like a Midwestern newscaster didn't mean they couldn't count or do differential calculus.

Wayne finally planted our first garden earlier that spring. It was huge. It produced so many vegetables that the kids invented excuses to avoid harvesting duty. Wayne and I were thrilled when the green beans and okra plants towered above us, and delighted in finding the inevitable hidden gigantic zucchini. The vegetables grew almost by the hour, and the result of a full day of sun was amazing to witness. We lunched on a microwave mix of fresh sliced yellow squash, onion, tomatoes, basil, and oregano.

Wayne said the big storm had knocked fruit off the side orchard, so we'd have fewer persimmons than expected. The kids grew up eating bright-orange persimmon slices, crowding their dad during story time to beg for more "simmons." Those days were gone. They were great kids, but they didn't crowd close to us anymore, for any reason.

I closed the heavy French glass office doors to leave the Saturday noise and bustle behind. It was rare for me to work weekends, but I needed to revise a training program I was presenting next week.

I'd worked from home as a management consultant since Christine was born. Our recent conversion of the formal dining and living rooms to offices created the ideal home office setting for Wayne and me. The French glass doors provided sound-proofing with a view between each office, plus I could easily see our entryway and Wayne had a view of the kitchen through the butler's pantry. The kids knew not to interrupt phone conversations but waved for attention when needed. The sound-proofing allowed the kids to listen to music, watch TV, or goof off after they got off the school bus, as we worked a bit longer. I was thrilled to work from home and have a quiet office to do so. While waiting for the desktop to power up, I brushed a speck of dust off the forest green marble inlaid at the center of my antique desk, another auction find.

Later that afternoon, I heard Wayne singing Bobby McFerrin's "Don't Worry, Be Happy" in the hall. He usually sang as he walked through the house. "The Bare Necessities" from Disney's *The Jungle Book* and "Baa Baa Black Sheep" were standbys when the kids were little, and his current playlist included The Commodores' "She's a Brick House," B.B. King's "The Thrill Is Gone," and "If I Were a Fat Man," his version of the song from *Fiddler on the Roof*. The kids loved hearing him sing, and his playlist reminded me that all was good in our world.

We'd worked hard to create a perfect setting for children. My psychology background and my own teen experience made me apprehensive about the terrifying minefields presented by the teen years. I was determined to provide a safe haven to allow our kids to navigate the potentially difficult years ahead. They did well in school, were involved in activities, and had friends they grew up with, all important elements for plotting a successful course through the teen years. Shelby would be a challenge, but we were as prepared as we could be.

I glanced at the plush carpet grass outside my office window, then spotted Shelby and two girlfriends riding bikes along the street. *Lord, have mercy, of course she's not holding the handlebars.* Shelby pedaled at an easy pace; her arms balanced straight to either side with her palms cupping the wind. Her friends trailed in a V formation like the foundation of any respectable parade, but the second-tier girls possessed enough sense—or fear—to grasp their handlebars. I'd warned Shelby to hold on because just one rock or one hole in the pavement could cause a fall, but she was undaunted. No matter how much I pushed for safety, she spirited along her own fearless path.

While I loved that our kids could play in the yard and ride their bikes without supervision, it took years for me to adapt to life in a small Texas town. After visiting Harrison's library and discovering the high school had advanced classes and a chess club, I assumed that a small town was a tiny version of the suburbs I'd experienced growing up in Maryland. After moving, I realized I missed sidewalks, museums, and restaurants. I made peace with my choice when Christine was three and Shelby an infant. I panicked after discovering Christine's bed empty and the garage door gaping open early one morning. I was about to combust into a puff of smoke when I spied a tiny body on the road a football field away. Christine marched purposefully, head held high and pudgy arms swinging wide on her journey home. My panic subsided when I realized she looked happy. After we hugged, Christine said last evening's teen babysitter said Christine could visit without her baby sister, so she'd dressed and left early that morning. Christine located the sitter's house down the street, knocked, opened the unlocked door, found the sitter's room, and crawled in bed with her.

Christine sighed, raised her tiny shoulders to her ears, then exhaled heavily. "She wouldn't wake up, so I came home."

All my complaints about lack of amenities disappeared. I hugged Christine, then we toasted 8 a.m. with waffles and syrup. While our small town wasn't perfect, it kept our curious three-year-old safe. I'd been grateful for that ever since.

Later Saturday afternoon, one day after the big rain, I paused from work to check the laundry. I smiled every time I walked through the computer area we created between the kitchen and den. The old walk-through utility room now featured a desk, chair, and the kids' computer screen facing out for adult scrutiny. The internet was new, and young users often ended up on the wrong website without trying. Based on walk-by scans, Shelby and Justin stuck with science games, math games, and *Where in the World Is Carmen Sandiego?*

That evening Justin and a friend watched *Shrek* in the den. Justin propped his leg on the couch while his friend relaxed in the recliner. A few weeks earlier I sewed four gigantic floor pillows with a purple, turquoise, and gold Route 66 scene, then piled them in a wicker basket for extra seating for additional friends—our remodeling was officially complete! Shelby spent the night at a friend's house, but Christine stayed home to study. Christine often went out with friends, but stayed home to catch up when homework and debate research was too demanding.

We were members of a small congregation with an intelligent, warm pastor, and if it was like the others, that Sunday's sermon was amazing. I'm sure I enjoyed it and expected to reflect on her message during the week. We probably chatted with friends after the service, gratefully noting the water subsiding from fields and ditches. Relieved to escape rain damage and having caught up on work, I was a bit on autopilot; it was time to relax and enjoy a lazy Sunday afternoon. We would have piled through the side door with groceries, Wayne singing, "Camptown ladies, sing this song," with the kids joining in on the "Doo dah, doo dah" refrain. (Years later, Justin sometimes still called his dad "Doo Dah.")

2

MONDAY MORNING DISCOVERY

The kids were out the door before 7 a.m. with our responsible oldest child behind the wheel. Wayne and I gladly relinquished daily school round trips when Christine became comfortable driving. I put on running shoes, poured cat food into bowls, then jogged around the neighborhood. Running lifted my mood and dampened my anxiety, so I circled the neighborhood daily after the kids left. The morning air smelled fresh after the rainy weekend. My mind cleared when I ran, and I loved the relaxing "cool down" walk afterward. I returned to the kitchen, then floured a pot roast, sprinkled it with salt and pepper, and seared it on all sides. After a few minutes, I added onion, garlic, and basil.

Wayne appeared as the onion caramelized. "The bathroom smells like mildew. Did you notice?"

"It's not that bad; I think it's okay." I've never been a fan of bad news, so I sometimes open with a denial, at least until more information arrives. It's not a coping mechanism to brag about, but a product of my lifelong relationship with anxiety. I still struggle to confine worry to potential problems that are real, immediate, and within my sphere of influence.

"It's pretty bad; come see." He walked toward the hall, then turned to wait. I stirred a large can of diced tomatoes into the pot, turned off the stove, then followed him.

A strong musty smell struck me as soon as I walked in our bathroom. I was shocked at the contrast to the fresh air I'd enjoyed during my run.

Imagine a basketball team's sweaty uniforms, damp socks, and wet towels left in a heap for two weeks in a warm locker room. The smell wasn't just sour, but moldy. I stood on my toes for better air, then realized I couldn't escape; the musty odor filled the room. Wayne told me to smell near the baseboard outside the shower. I reluctantly leaned down and halfheartedly sniffed.

My throat immediately constricted and I jerked away. "That smells awful!"

Wayne frowned. "It's really bad!"

I trailed my finger along the smooth grout outlining the small ceramic tiles. "I can't see mold or mildew anywhere. That doesn't seem possible given how strong it smells."

"It must be inside the wall. I'll remove the baseboards and spray underneath with Clorox."

I inspected the shower wall, searching for visible clues. *How could the stench be so overpowering when yesterday there was no odor at all? The leak was early Saturday morning and it's only Monday morning. How could it smell this bad when we couldn't find any growth or discoloration?*

After my release from smelling duties, I was relieved to breathe the hallway's clean air and the kitchen's fragrant onion, garlic, and basil aroma. I reflected as I stirred in beef broth and red wine, then lowered the stove to simmer. Bad news had to break through my self-protective filter before it could be processed and seize space from other worries. Once inside, though, potential problems received loads of focus, and herculean amounts of thought. In emergencies, I jump into action; I simply cannot sit when there is a clear solution to follow. While the smell was very bad, Wayne had an excellent solution. I was concerned but completely confident Wayne would resolve our smelly problem.

Wayne and I were fixers. I thrived in the corporate world of projects, deadlines and agendas, and he excelled in the physical world of building, maintaining, and fixing. I was totally confident that, between the two of us, we could solve anything. I sat at my desk, punched the CD player remote and leaned toward my keyboard as *Fiddler on the Roof* played in the background.

The next morning Wayne started on the bathroom. I promised to check the internet to see how to address mold after I finished some work. I was presenting a new pre-employment selection process to Human Resources managers on Friday. After spending two years overseeing test and interview development, I was excited to begin the implementation process.

Late that afternoon Wayne appeared in my office doorway, drenched with sweat. His face was flushed and he looked exhausted. He shoved his facemask to his forehead and announced, "There's black mold behind the shower tile."

My jaw dropped. While we expected to find mold, I was shocked he found black mold, supposedly the worst kind.

Wayne wiped sweat off his face with his shirttail. "I tore out part of the shower wall. I double-bagged the wall and insulation and put it in the trash." He leaned against the doorframe and frowned. "I should have worn gloves. Just handling it made me throw up. I started having bad diarrhea after thirty minutes, but had to keep working." He paused, then looked at me. "This stuff is really awful. It's clearly dangerous, since it immediately made me that sick."

I nodded, but didn't fully comprehend his words. I'd never heard of getting diarrhea and vomiting after touching something.

I followed Wayne to our bathroom, which now looked like a demolition project. The toilet and shower door were gone. The baseboard along the shower wall was gone, as was the bottom few feet of sheetrock. The shower walls next to the toilet, along the back of the shower, and along the exterior of the house were intact and still covered with one-inch ceramic tiles. Wayne said the mold would dry up now that air could circulate around the shower wall opening. Once it dried, our air would get better.

By Wednesday—two days later—the air was much worse. I couldn't take a deep breath in our bedroom, and instinctively resorted to short, shallow breaths. Without realizing it, I had turned into a mouth-breather; my nose couldn't handle the workload. I was forced to inhale and exhale through my mouth.

I mouth-breathed down the hall to see if it had spread to Justin's and Shelby's rooms. No mold was visible, but the smell was there also. I walked through our living room and offices, seeking comfort in familiar surroundings.

Everything looked normal.

Unfortunately, the living room and offices smelled awful as well, but not as bad as our bedroom. I was shocked and frightened at how completely the mold overtook our air in only two days.

At lunch I stated the obvious, "The smell is worse now."

Wayne winced. "I know. I'll knock an inspection hole in the exterior wall of the house outside the shower, then use that to pull out part of the shower wall. Apparently, I didn't get it all yet. Once I remove the source, our air will get better."

Hours later Wayne appeared in my office doorway, his

sweat-soaked shirt clinging to his chest. He raised his arms above his head and touched his fingers together, then slowly dropped them down at an angle, saying, "There is a giant black Christmas tree of black mold as big as a man on all three walls of the shower." He pushed his mask further up on his head, and said he'd removed and double bagged most of the shower tile and sheetrock.

Wayne said it was possible the tile grout had never been sealed, allowing water to seep behind the tile onto water-resistant green board for years. We preferred baths, so the shower wasn't used daily. He guessed the small leak from the nineteen-inch rain set off mold that had been growing behind the shower tile for years. He said he didn't know this for sure, and the cause wasn't our immediate concern because we had to focus on getting it fixed.

Wayne looked exhausted. "I don't think I can fix this by myself. I've reached my limit on what I can do. We need to get help."

I was shocked. I'd never, in seventeen years of marriage, heard Wayne admit defeat, especially regarding fixing something.

He was fascinated by machines and loved to build things. I'd learned years ago not to expect to enjoy the radio while driving past a construction site. Instead, I'd receive an unsolicited running commentary on building techniques, materials, project status, and equipment. This man knew how to build and fix most anything.

If he said he needed help, then we needed help.

Wayne smiled weakly and sank down in the doorway, saying he'd check to see if we still had mold coverage. He said most insurance companies stopped covering mold because it was so expensive, and he thought he got a letter to that effect a few months ago. He said he'd call our agent Monday morning.

He stared at the floor, then back up at me. "I've done everything I can, and it just gets worse."

My jaw dropped. In seventeen years of marriage, I'd also never heard Wayne give up—especially when it came to fixing something. I rushed to reassure him, saying he'd done everything possible and the insurance company would know how to get rid of mold. I hoped we had mold coverage, but even if we didn't, certainly they'd provide information on how to fix our home. Wayne had done all he could. We needed expertise, expertise I was certain they'd provide.

Thursday night I couldn't breathe our thick bedroom air without making a conscious effort to draw breath in, then push it back out. It was frightening, having to focus in order to fill and empty my lungs. I was afraid I could die if I fell asleep and couldn't intentionally draw air, then purposefully push it back out. I lay there, struggling for air, then realized the bedroom wasn't safe.

I touched Wayne's shoulder and whispered, "I can't breathe in here. I'm going to sleep in Shelby's room. Do you want to move too?"

He didn't budge, but mumbled he was fine where he was.

I climbed in Shelby's extra bunk-bed. The air stunk there as well but at least I could breathe.

I woke early Friday, showered in Christine's bathroom, and then wrapped in a towel. When I stepped in our bedroom, I felt tiny electric sparks explode randomly across my wet scalp...pop, pop, pop! The popping felt like mild pinpricks, and increased with each step toward our bathroom. Somehow my wet scalp had the right conditions to sprout the mold spores that packed our air. By the time I faced the mirror my head supported an eruption of miniature fireworks...pop, pop, pop, my personal

July fourth finale. The popping increased to such intensity that I was temporarily mesmerized. I leaned toward the mirror and parted my hair to inspect my scalp.

Unable to see anything but a wet scalp, I snapped back to reality. Fireworks or no, I had a sixty-mile commute and an eight-hour training program to present. I turned on the hairdryer and was relieved that the popping slowed as my hair dried. The popping ceased after I was on the freeway with the AC on full blast.

It was a poor choice to spend time in a moldy bathroom with wet hair; I reeked of wet socks all day. I couldn't believe I had perfectly mimicked Pig-Pen from *Peanuts*. Instead of dirt, I was surrounded by a thick cloud of stinky spores. I was mortified to smell like damp trash in a spotless corporate setting. Every time someone leaned over to talk to me, I reflexively stepped back, leaving a pungent odor in my wake. No one mentioned the smell, so I'll never know if they didn't notice or were simply too polite to inquire about my interesting perfume or ask when musk oil regained popularity.

It was dark when I got home. The kids had eaten and dispersed, so Wayne joined me at the table. I was tired and hungry, so I shoveled my dinner while Wayne told me he'd called our insurance agent at InsureUS. Our agent said the company would review our policy and claim dates to determine if they would cover our claim, then he'd contact an adjuster to come out to inspect the bathroom.

My shoulders relaxed. "That's great; we need expert advice!"

"He said it's our responsibility to take reasonable action to protect our property."

Alarmed, I put down my spoon to focus on Wayne. "Did he tell you what we should do?"

"No, he didn't. But I mentioned things I did, like cleaning with a Clorox solution and opening up the wall to let it dry out. He agreed those were good ideas, but said we need to do everything possible to get this corrected."

I was concerned about the lack of direction about "reasonable action," but pleased that Wayne's efforts were blessed by our agent. With Wayne's flexible farming and ranching schedule, he'd focused full-time effort to fix this problem, something most homeowners couldn't do. Feeling heartened by food and reassuring news, I said, "We'll research it tomorrow. You said ozone generators might kill mold since they're used to sterilize equipment. I'll locate the top generators for you to compare."

I searched the internet for "mold" and "mold treatment" on Saturday morning. There wasn't solid data to support claims that ozone would eradicate mold. Instead, the computer screen was splashed with bright yellow and red promises such as "100% Guaranteed" or "Home and Industrial Use." I clicked on different ads, then got lost in disturbing displays of orange mold, hairy mold, tan mold, white mold, fuzzy mold, black mold, and more.

Several factors impacted our ability to collect quality information about mold back then. First of all, mold cleanup information wasn't readily available. While there were plenty of internet ads promising results, in 2002 there wasn't guidance from governmental, environmental, or even self-help groups to help separate fact from bogus sales claims. This meant my search produced little more than product ads with flashy promises. It was frustrating as I tried locating helpful products among the flashy claims.

Second, and more frightening, I realized I couldn't comprehend what I was reading; I couldn't concentrate or process information. Hunching toward the screen didn't help, and neither did several deep breaths or a caffeine break. I stood up, circled the room several times, then sat down to discover that yes, indeed,

I was *still stupid*. I had a headache and couldn't think, at all. I remember scanning the room for answers as I wondered why I couldn't understand what I read.

I became worried when I realized the mold toxins affected my ability to think. *How can we make reasonable choices if we can't process information?*

I felt foolish ordering an ozone generator; it felt like buying the modern-day equivalent of snake oil. But we had to take action, so Wayne selected an expensive industrial strength generator. I didn't want to spend nine hundred dollars on an ozone generator, but we were in a fight to save our home. Whatever the cost, we had to do what was necessary.

We pushed through our mental fog to make decisions. Looking back, we were exhausted from trying to focus in my mold-infested office; it took everything we had to read the words on the screen, much less comprehend them. I'm guessing I was reading at a fifth-grade level at that point. When I wasn't laser-focused on trying to comprehend, I alternated between frustration and fear that I couldn't think like I normally could. It was incredibly frightening not to be able to think clearly or concentrate. *If I can't think, then I can't work. I need to think to make critical decisions about how to solve this crisis.* To compound my fear, I didn't know how long my cognitive impairment would last, if it would get worse, and whether our kids would be affected.

Wayne created a remediation shopping list: facemasks, gloves, air purifiers with HEPA (high-efficiency particulate air) filters, bleach, and Clorox wipes. Some internet sources said ultraviolet light would kill mold, so he added black lights for treating clothes hanging in the closet. Walmart was forty minutes away in the next town. We took the kids along and planned to enjoy Chinese food after shopping.

The kids were excited to eat out, and were oblivious to the seriousness of our situation. I was relieved they weren't impacted, but worried how much longer that would be possible. They were enthralled with the Chinese Zodiac animals lining the paper place-mats, and, as usual, teased Wayne and me about our signs. Shelby and Justin chanted softly, "Mommy's a monkey, Mommy's a monkey!" I remember struggling to act engaged and smiling weakly at their chatter. On the way home the girls' backseat singing peaked with a long, drawn-out version of Whitney Houston's "And…I…will…always love YOU!" while Justin begged to listen to anything else or nothing at all. So life remained fairly normal for our children.

Wayne got up early Sunday morning to remove the rest of the shower wall. He declined my offer to help, "You don't want to mess with this stuff; it's really, really bad. I may leave the exterior opening uncovered so the heat will help it dry out."

And it was hot. Fall and spring weren't readily identifiable in our corner of the Texas Gulf Coast. Our default weather was hot and humid, except for enthusiastic thunder paired with drenching rain, until winter revealed chillier days. A few days produced several options: hot and humid, followed by thunder-storms, and finishing with a blast of cold air. It was impossible to dress young children for school, and more than one mother semi-worried about CPS visits after sending first graders off in shorts and T-shirts, only to have them sprint off the school bus shivering and shrieking only hours later. Eternally clueless, we improvised with jacket-stuffed backpacks for most of the school year.

Our mid-September forecast was 92 degrees with 76 percent humidity, which was rather dry for our area. I opened the doors and windows to air out the house, then shooed our cats and the neighbor's dogs away from the open doors.

In just one week, my life had progressed from a steady trot with time for breaks to a full-on gallop to save our home.

3

HOW LONG WILL WE SLEEP IN THE LIVING ROOM?

On Monday, I moved several work outfits to the laundry room at the far side of the house so I'd have odor-free clothing for future work meetings. The mold was gaining on us quicker than I thought possible. I was devastated when the insurance adjuster pushed our appointment back three days, so I called to persuade him to come earlier. My carefully selected words painted a clear picture of our deteriorating home while remaining calm and factual. I told him we could hardly breathe in our bedrooms and I was worried about our kids and our health.

I wanted to tell him the mold diminished my ability to think, but I didn't want to sound like I was overreacting. I needed his help. For that to happen, he had to visit. Only one week into this ordeal and I was already monitoring my words to avoid being dismissed as crazy. Just a week in, and it was clear we were in for a wild ride.

I waited until the door slammed a third time Tuesday morning, signaling the kids had left for school and it was safe to talk freely. I took another sip of coffee, then broached the focus of my every waking hour, our living situation. "I can't sleep in our bedroom; I can't even breathe in there."

Wayne stared down at his Dr Pepper can, possibly waiting for superpowers or the caffeine and sugar blend to kick in.

"None of us should sleep back there. I'm worried we may not wake up," I insisted.

It didn't take long to drag four twin mattresses from Shelby's bunkbed and Justin's trundle to the living room, transforming it into the "before" slumber party picture.

Justin and Shelby appeared unfazed by the mattress-packed living room when they returned from school. Justin scanned the room and dropped his backpack on a mattress. "How long will we sleep in here?"

I was thrilled at his casualness and wondered how long he'd remain that way. Without a fact-based answer, I said I wasn't sure but we'd sleep there until the bedroom area was fixed. He grinned, stretched his arms wide, then fell forward on his chosen mattress. Justin viewed this as an adventure, an attitude I hoped to adopt as my theme for the coming months.

On Wednesday Wayne set up the ozone generator in our bedroom and said he'd turn on the bathroom heater while the generator ran. He looked over and added, "I need to uncover the bathroom ceiling vent I covered last week."

I stared up at the vent, then directed my gaze back to Wayne. "You can't uncover it. Spores will move to the attic once you uncover that vent."

Wayne exhaled slowly. "Mold's probably already there. The spores are so small they can go anywhere." He paused. "Besides, we ran the central air to dry the house out; we had to do that, remember?"

I nodded. We'd debated running the AC, then decided we had to do something to lower the indoor humidity.

Satisfied that the vent debate was over, Wayne added, "I'll run the heater to reduce the humidity more. Hopefully that will kill the mold."

We had to do something—the musty smell was overwhelming. Mold spores had definitely found their way throughout the house. Wayne uncovered the vent, turned up the heat, and ran the attic fan to circulate the air. We hoped the combination of ozone and high heat would kill the spores. Based on our research, ozone was bad for mold, people, and electronics. We covered our electronics and left the house while the ozone generator ran.

A few days later, we met John, our insurance adjuster. Young and lanky, John wore a crisp yellow shirt and khakis. I was surprised he didn't bring a mask. We dodged twin mattresses as we walked through the living room, then opened our bedroom door.

John frowned as the stench met him at the door. "Much worse back here, isn't it?"

Wayne and I looked at each other, wide-eyed. If he thought our bedroom was bad, I wondered what he'd say when he smelled the bathroom air.

John made notes on his clipboard as he inspected the shower remnants. He kept glancing at the door as he questioned Wayne, then asked if we could finish talking outside. He clearly wanted out of our moldy bathroom and house. We felt the same way.

Once outside, John faced us. "Based on what I've seen, I'm confident we'll cover your claim."

I was elated; I couldn't stop grinning or even remain still. I tried to control my excitement, but I'm pretty sure I hopped from one foot to the other. I was certain the worst was over now that we had help.

John glanced at his clipboard. "You need to have the house tested to determine what type of mold you have, and where it is. The testing company will provide a plan to remediate, or clean, your house based on that information." John paused for this to sink in. "The remediation company will follow the testing protocol to clean your house."

"Can the same company do our testing and remediation?" Wayne asked.

"No, it must be two independent companies," John responded.

"Okay. Will you tell us who to use?" I wrote September 21 at the top of my notepad and waited for contact information.

John shook his head. "No, we can't be involved in your selection of firms."

"How will we find a good firm? There are horror stories about remediation companies taking your money and leaving." I wondered how we would avoid missteps without guidance.

"Do your research—there are good firms around," John continued. "After testing and remediation, you'll get the house tested again. Hopefully, it will test clean and you can rebuild."

I skipped ahead. "Can we stay here during the process?"

"In some situations people stay in their houses; other times they have to move until the house tests clean." He glanced at our back door, then at us. "Based on what I saw here, I think you'll need to move out."

"Move out?" I was stunned. "Where will we go? There aren't rent houses around here. We live in a small town. Even if we found a rent house, it won't fit all of us." I struggled to keep up with this twist in the conversation.

"If they tell you to move that means your house isn't fit to live in, so you'll have to move." John winced. "It's pretty unpleasant in there. You should start looking at options."

I knew John was right, but I had no idea where we'd go. I started my to-do list: Get mold testing done, find a place to live, research and select a remediation firm. I took notes as John explained the process, saying we'd receive a living allowance from the insurance company, plus replacement costs for ruined items.

Wayne perked up. "So the cost to rebuild the shower will be covered?"

"Exactly. Or if the testing company tells you to throw things away, like toiletries or food. The insurance company will pay to replace damaged items."

"How do we know what needs to be replaced?" My pen raced across the page.

"We'll let you know after we get the remediation, or cleaning, protocol from the testing company. Everything will be spelled out in the remediation plan," John said.

My mind jumped ahead to Thanksgiving. I asked John how long the process would take.

"It's too early to say. It might take a month but might be longer depending on the type of mold and scope of the problem." John started toward his car, then turned back. "You may want to put plastic sheeting over your hallway to seal those bedrooms from the rest of the house."

"But we need things from there. Clothes, medicine, kids' stuff; everything is back there. How will we access our stuff?" I asked.

"You can still get items; just close it up afterwards," John called as he walked to his car.

After school, Shelby ran her fingers along the taped edges of the heavy plastic sheeting covering the hallway entrance. She inched an opening in the overlapping sheets to peer down the hall, then glanced over to ask if she could get things from her room. I said she and Justin could retrieve what they needed, but to wear a facemask in the hallway or their bedrooms. I said they should move through the barrier quickly and keep trips to a minimum by gathering several items at a time.

I tried to sound matter-of-fact when adding, "From now on we'll all use Christine's bathroom." I didn't mention that our shower was demolished and they'd be covered by popping mold spores if they showered in their bathroom. My goal was to shield them as long as possible while we worked to get our house back to normal.

Fall was Christine's busiest time of year with football and volleyball games, so she wasn't home much and was preoccupied when she was home. We exchanged scheduling updates at night and before school, and I continued reassuring her we'd get help fixing the house. Swamped with cheerleading, band, debate research, and other activities, she asked few questions before returning to homework.

The plastic sheeting didn't halt the mold's spread as expected. In fact, it didn't appear to slow the spread at all. Three weeks and three days after the big rain, we lost the living room, kitchen, and both offices. The mold moved faster than we could adapt. In three weeks, three-fourths of our house was so contaminated we couldn't occupy those rooms.

Our air looked like thick clear Jell-O. A heavy mist of mold particles glistened in the morning sunlight streaming through our office windows. Tiny shimmering spores hung suspended in the air, each bumped up next to its neighbor. I waved my hand to scatter the spores, but they didn't budge. The bumped spores wiggled, but held firmly in their suspended locations. I couldn't see them without direct sunlight, but if our office air was full, then so was the back of the house.

That night I transferred my meeting notes with the adjuster to a spiral binder, then added dates and details about the big rain, the smells, and Wayne's remediation efforts. I wanted to document our efforts to fix our home.

Wayne and I were completely focused on finding solutions. Our immediate need was a safe place to sleep; then we'd concentrate on a clean place to eat and work. Interactions outside these goals didn't receive my consideration, so I didn't fully grasp Wayne's extreme physical pain. I heard him say a water moccasin appeared next to his truck while he fed cattle at the ranch. I understood he reached back for the shotgun so quickly that he broke a rib. But his pain didn't really sink in. I was in survival mode, with my sole focus getting our family to a safe place. Everything else was noise competing for space in my overwrought brain.

Under siege, we escaped to our final refuge—the newly remodeled section of our home: the den, Christine's room, and Christine's bathroom at the furthest end of the house. Hoping against reason and experience, Wayne carefully taped a plastic barrier over the doorway between the kitchen and den.

Wayne and I told Christine to stay in her room that night to rest before the SAT exam, then quietly slid three twin mattresses past her closed door to the den. There was barely room to walk after we crammed mattresses next to the loveseat. It was impossible to sleep after Wayne began snoring loudly, one of his superpowers.

I woke hearing Justin groggily plead, "Dad, please stop *snoring!*"

I didn't realize Shelby was awake until she snapped from the loveseat, "Shut up, Justin, he can't even hear you!" They bickered for a few minutes, Justin sleepily and Shelby firing on all cylinders, then quieted as Wayne's snoring continued unabated. It was a laughable, pitiful scene.

The next morning Wayne teased Christine about living like a queen, sleeping alone in her double bed in the next room. Mortified that we'd camped outside her bedroom, Christine asked why we didn't send Shelby to sleep with her. I said she needed her sleep since she was taking the SAT. She protested that we still should have sent Shelby to sleep with her.

Wayne and I took turns rustling through the plastic barrier to grab yogurt, milk, and cereal for their breakfast. We no longer allowed the kids in the kitchen or the back of the house for any reason, no exceptions. Once Wayne and I realized we couldn't think after being exposed to the mold, the kids were banned from those areas.

I held my breath while pulling bowls from the kitchen cabinet. The kitchen air was horrible, worse than hot, wet, dumpster air. I concentrated to perform the immediate task at hand, feeding our children and sending them to school, while intentionally inhaling and exhaling depending on my location.

I exhaled as I pushed open the clear plastic sheeting while clutching spoons and yogurt containers. I surveyed the mattress-stuffed den and was struck by how surreal our life was. Schools send home instructions for test-day preparation, reminding parents to provide their kids with a good night's sleep, healthy breakfast, minimal stress, and a positive start to the day. Frustrated at my inability to provide such things, I thought, *I have a Ph.D. in Industrial/Organizational Psychology. I design pre-employment tests for a multinational company and write testing tips to prepare applicants for test day. I don't need tips on how to prepare my kids for testing; this content is firmly within my wheelhouse.* Yet my children were living in an uncertain, unhealthy, crowded, and stressful home environment, spooning from Yoplait containers on the way to school and the SAT. This wasn't my plan for our children's test-day or school-day preparation. This was the first of many times that the life I'd worked for and planned for differed dramatically from the life we were living. I would spend many months fighting to close the gap between these two lives, and trying to minimize my expectations as the gap grew.

It wasn't that my life always met my expectations or that I'd never had disappointments, it's just that I'd worked hard and thus far had managed to ensure that my children had what they needed to succeed and thrive, with the foundation being a safe, healthy home. And suddenly, on SAT day, it became clear the life we created had vanished.

With the kids gone, Wayne and I leaned mattresses against the wall and sat on the loveseat to discuss what to do. Our house had deteriorated so quickly we couldn't keep up.

"I'm really worried. I can't work in my office." I winced before revealing the depth of my fear, "Wayne, I can't focus; I can't even think in there."

Wayne slowly nodded while staring at the floor tile. "I didn't want you to worry, but you need to know it's definitely affected me."

He hunched forward and slowly exhaled. "I can't count to ten."

I frowned. "What do you mean you can't count to ten? Of course you can count!"

He slowly shook his head. "No, I can't. Not in a way that matters."

Wayne took a deep breath. "I tried to count irrigation equipment a few days ago. I need a count to expand irrigation at the ranch. You know those ten-inch steel valves, each as big as a gallon milk jug?"

He pointed at the baseboard on our right, "They're stacked outside the garage wall."

He stood up, shoulders bowed forward, as he gazed down at the imaginary collection of metal cylinders. "So I start counting. They're in groups, three to five deep from the wall."

His raised eyebrows caught my attention as he added, "Only one layer high."

Staring at the imaginary pile, he whispered, "I count a few, but when I step to the next section, I can't remember which ones I counted." He grimaced. "So I start over."

Wayne leaned toward the pile. "I try to focus. I point at each one. I count out loud."

He raised his finger toward the baseboard, "One."

"Two, three." With each number, his finger tracked along the floor.

He stepped left, then pointed at the baseboard, "Four."

Slowly, his arm dropped down. He turned toward me, his eyes filled with pain, "Every time I get to eight or nine, I lose track."

He stepped back to the right and scowled at the baseboard, "I have to start over again!"

Wayne collapsed beside me, leaned over, and put his head in his hands. "I *still* don't know how many valves I have."

Jaw clenched, his frustration clear, he added, "So, no, I can't even *fucking* count to ten!"

I shut my eyes to block his terrifying news. Wayne was one of the smartest people I knew. It was impossible to imagine he couldn't count, but understandable that he couldn't recall enough to keep track while counting. He'd told me many times the mold impacted his ability to focus and remember. I had the same problem; I couldn't think enough to work in my office.

I was stunned as his disclosure sunk in, *We'll never find*

our way out of this mess if we can't think. How can we navigate through this chaos if we can't reason or remember what we are doing? Our mold foe was mighty, and we'd need every ounce of smarts to beat it. If we couldn't think, we were doomed to fail.

I stewed for a moment. "This must be what happens. People with mold get stupider and stupider. They finally get too stupid to leave. Then they die."

Wayne's face was still hidden in his hands. "This is bad shit. We have to get out of here." He hadn't budged at all.

My concern switched to our children. "Do you think it's affecting the kids?" I cringed. "If so, Christine can forget a National Merit scholarship; she'll be lucky to bubble her name in correctly." My giggle erupted from fear and the shock of how quickly our lives had deteriorated.

Wayne considered my question before responding. "I think the kids are fine. I haven't noticed any problems. They're in school all day, so their exposure is limited."

"Thank goodness." I paused. "The damage isn't permanent, right?"

"I don't think so. I can think clearly after spending the day at the ranch."

"That's good." I nodded. "But long-term exposure can't be healthy for any of us."

Wayne grimaced. "Of course not. We have to get out of here. It is really scary."

"I didn't know mold could cause problems with thinking or memory. It's so frightening." I was overwhelmed as the enormity of our situation continued to sink in.

Wayne pointed at the plastic-covered door opening, eight steps away. "I don't know how long that barrier will hold it. When the spores get past the plastic, this air will be as bad as the rest of the house. We're down to the final corner of our home."

Before we knew it, the day was over. Best I can remember we remained huddled forward, caught in our worry, all day. I know we were still there, trying not to drool, when the back door swung open and flooded the room with fresh air and the blinding afternoon sun.

Justin stopped cold in the doorway, "Ewww. It really stinks in here!"

MOLD TESTING

Three TESTX environmental testers arrived Friday morning. They asked if the house was unlocked, then started toward the door without masks, suits, or shoe covers. Wayne asked if they had suits or facemasks, and they shook their heads no.

"It's bad in there. Do you want to use our masks?" Wayne asked.

The two young men said mold didn't bother them, then chuckled when the woman said she wanted a mask. Wayne asked what was funny about using a facemask, and one coworker said they called her "the canary" because she was the first to notice if the air was bad.

Wayne gave the woman a facemask and they disappeared inside. We peppered them with questions when they returned hours later. I wanted to know if our house was similar or worse than other houses they'd tested. The testers said we'd have to wait for the report, then hopped in their vehicles. I was disappointed they didn't tell us anything. I understood having to wait for official results, but was desperate for information about what was happening in the rooms where we worked and slept.

We sat on the pavement and leaned against the back door.

I watched their car slow, then turn away from our driveway. "They didn't change shoes or even wipe them off. I thought they'd put their shoes in a bag in the back of the truck. They didn't change shirts or anything!"

Wayne shook his head in disbelief. "It's the damnedest thing. Even we know mold spores hang on clothes, shoes, and hair; waiting to find a damp place to grow."

"So why don't mold testers—people in the industry—worry about this? How can they be comfortable dragging our spores to their cars and homes? If they have a leak in their home our mold spores will take over their house, just like here," I added.

None of this made sense. Mold caused memory problems and inability to focus—it happened to us. Mold could become airborne and take over a house in days—it happened to us. So how could professionals, those who were trained to work with mold daily, be nonchalant around unidentified mold?

On Monday I called a realtor to locate a rent house. She told me there wouldn't be any three-bedroom rent houses, much less a four-bedroom house, but she'd check. I asked her to look for houses to buy as well. We didn't *want* to buy another house, but we were desperate to find a clean place to live. Most of the homes in our small town were occupied; there were few vacancies of any kind. If the only safe place to sleep was via a home purchase, we might have to consider it. Like incurring debt to care for a sick child, we'd do what was necessary to protect our children. We were able, if far from eager, to spend our way out of this problem.

We learned years ago that saving was critical for entrepreneurs without a stable income. The 1986 oil bust hit us hard, arriving in tandem with our first baby and the first year of our new businesses. Wayne had just started the turf grass farm when I began working as an independent consultant. To reconcile our small income and huge farm expenses, the three of us lived in an apartment built inside a barn on our grass farm. We lived there until we could afford our current home, where we continued saving for future surprises.

I called apartment complexes to see what was available. After discussing floor plans, I ventured into my primary focus. "My oldest daughter has lots of after-school activities, and often comes home late. What is security like there?"

The manager's response floored me. "We don't discuss 'security' in the apartment industry. It's just not a topic we talk about."

I was so stunned I couldn't respond. I thanked her and hung up, wondering why they couldn't discuss lighting, trimmed shrubs, call boxes, or a neighborhood watch? I shuddered at the thought of Christine returning to a dark parking lot at 1 a.m. after a football game. So apartments might not be a solution either.

As expected, there weren't any viable rent houses. Wayne and I visited a few homes for sale, then decided it was too early to consider buying another home just three weeks after the mold explosion. Over lunch, Wayne described a bed and breakfast an acquaintance was remodeling. It was a beautiful old three-story plantation-style house with huge covered porches and a big kitchen. The renovation was costly and lengthier than expected, and the house was not quite ready for guests.

Wayne sipped iced tea. "Maybe we could rent it while she finishes remodeling. We'll fix our house in a month or so. When we move she'll be ready for real guests."

Wayne said the bed and breakfast was forty-five minutes from our house, but only twenty-five minutes from Christine's high school. The B&B was located in a remote, peaceful location. We'd have three bedrooms and two bathrooms, which was certainly workable. Wayne said he'd known Kim, the B&B owner for years.

Wayne beamed. "She's really nice. Remember I told you I stopped by on my way home from the ranch to see how the remodeling was going?"

"That sounds wonderful, but it's so far away. Let's look closer to home first."

We lingered after lunch to delay returning to our unlivable home. I felt human spending time around non-overwhelmed people and relaxed in their presence. The worn linoleum tile and fluorescent lighting were hardly upscale, but the air was deliciously clean.

That afternoon I spoke with an apartment manager who assured me her complex was very safe. They only had two-bedroom apartments, but I figured the kids could sleep in bunkbeds in one room. Not an ideal arrangement, but "ideal" had left our conversations quite a while ago. I made an appointment to visit with Shelby and Justin after school.

Friends of Shelby called out as we crossed the parking lot, "Heeeyy girl, what you doing here?"

"Heeyyy! We might move here," Shelby yelled as she sprinted toward the group.

The group buzzed with updates. "Awesome! Veronica and Sam live here too! Want to come hang with Sam and my brother Anthony? Anthony's in tenth grade and he's super cool."

Shelby was positively electric with excitement; I thought she would combust right there. I told her she couldn't hang out with them because we had to look at apartments together. We walked through the two-bedroom apartment, then left. There was no way I'd keep her out of trouble with hallways filled with doors to knock on and interesting people behind each one. The only reason she missed her midnight rendezvous last year was because her ride never arrived to pick her up. Apartments removed an important margin of safety for a gregarious, fearless pre-teen—she could disappear in minutes from an apartment. Apartment life was not a good option with young Shelby.

On Friday, Wayne moved my computer, printer, and phone to Christine's room. I was so excited to get back to work, I hovered over him as he hooked up the equipment.

I remained blissfully engaged with work until late that afternoon when Wayne said the adjuster called with our test results. Wayne paused. "Our house has toxic mold."

My hand reflexively covered my gaping mouth as Wayne continued. "Our bathroom and bedroom have toxic mold. All our contents need to be cleaned."

Wayne paused. "Even the kitchen has toxic mold. All the cabinets must be completely removed."

"The kitchen has toxic mold as well? How did it get to the kitchen on the other side of the house?" I wondered aloud.

"I have no idea, but it's toxic there as well." Wayne looked up from his notes. "John said we have to evacuate immediately."

"Oh my God." I shuddered. "Immediately?"

"Yes. He said it's not safe to live here."

Even though I knew our air was terrible, it was shocking to hear the term "toxic" applied to our home. It was frightening to hear a professional report that the house we slept in last night was unsafe. Not only that, but we'd sleep in our unsafe, toxic house again that night. I was mulling over the "unsafe house" declaration when I realized Wayne was saying the insurance company would cover our living costs while our house was remediated.

Wayne continued, "John said it will take at least a week for the full testing report, and additional time for the remediation plan. The remediation will take a minimum of thirty days, then the build back will take at least two weeks."

"The whole thing could be over in two months?" I smiled. "We could be back home by Thanksgiving?"

Wayne sighed. "I hope so."

The next morning Wayne made a deal with Kim, then told me we'd move later that evening.

Things never happened quickly, or without dialogue, at our house. Wayne and I didn't take a vacation, much less move, without many conversations. We'd never move without my seeing the new house, and he wouldn't arrange a move without discussing it with me first. But our home, where we slept and ate and worked, was toxic, so much of our normal process went out the window. This was an emergency, a hitch up in front of the plow and pull experience, like we'd never encountered. His behavior was unusual, but I was relieved he'd quickly solved our problem. I realized this might become our new norm, that we'd be pushed into more action and less discussion in the coming months. I'd never relinquish control under normal conditions, but found it easy in an emergency. Besides, no matter what the bed and breakfast looked like, any choice was better than a toxic home.

Wayne said, "Tell the kids to pick clothes for a week, then wash them in Consan 20."

"Where do I get Consan 20?"

"It's a fungicide you can buy at the feed store. I've used it at the farm before. It kills mold and it's safe for laundry. Hospitals and nursing homes use it to disinfect the laundry."

It was a blessing that not only did we pull our fair share in the marriage, but we never questioned each other's effort or decision-making. If Wayne felt he had an answer or a solution, I believed him. If I said I'd handle something, he knew I'd do it.

Looking back, it was impressive how effortlessly we handed the reins over to each other without a word. Of course we'd had rough spots in our marriage. I remember giggling toddlers swarming our legs after a particularly weighty argument. I lifted my gaze from the beaming child glued to my leg as he did the same, but his jaw hardened when our eyes met. I whispered above their blond curls that I would never leave them, and he matched my words and tone. Our fresh anger gave way to the realization that whether on the same team or miserably alone, both of us were staying. Not romance-novel material, but functional, and our respect, love, and trust continued to grow. Minor tiffs or "your-way/my-way" skirmishes wouldn't drain energy from our joint goal of getting our family to a safe, healthy home. We knew that despite our differences, we pulled for the same team. We respected each other's unique skills, knowledge, and views.

I marveled at the breadth of Wayne's knowledge as I drove to the feed store. He knew a little bit, and sometimes a lot, about a lot of things. What he didn't know, he learned by listening, questioning, watching, and doing. Since our insurance company didn't provide any information on how to safely move out—not a book, pamphlet, or checklist—his knowledge was critical to our survival. While his explicit painstaking attention to detail sometimes drove me crazy, this knowledge might just save us in a wasteland of absent guidance.

Luckily, move-out day was one of the four cool, crisp, sunny days allotted to the Texas Gulf Coast every autumn. I had missed the leaf-crunching brisk days of the East Coast since arriving in Texas two decades earlier, but was grateful for Saturday's brisk reproduction, with the welcome addition of our fierce Texas sun.

I told the kids to gather what they'd need and bring it to the driveway for inspection per Wayne's instruction. Three days' worth of clothing in one pile, two weeks' worth of clothing in another, and all other necessities were laid out to bake in the sun. We only allowed items that we could wash or wipe down, like fabric, metal, or plastic. We'd done lots of reading and were concerned about bringing mold spores to the B&B. If we carried spores with us to a location with a water leak, we could unintentionally seed another mold colony.

I took everything out of my purse, then wiped each item off and laid them in the sun to dry. I wished I could put our entire house outside; our blistering Texas sun would certainly destroy all mold spores. Wayne wiped off his leather belt and wallet. I even cleaned the prongs of my engagement ring, which was overkill because I'd been a dutiful hand washer since childhood; mold spores couldn't possibly live on my ring. We were obsessed with being thorough.

Justin asked who would feed our cats. I assured him that Dad and I would work in the detached garage most days and we'd leave extra food in the garage. We always left the garage door open a little so Meow Meow, Sassy, and Shadow could get food and shelter as desired. It wouldn't be a dramatic change for them.

We loaded the clothes in plastic trash bags and double-bagged them. The kids were volunteering at the Lions Club Festival booth all day. I washed clothes at the laundromat while they played and worked.

Christine later told me it was exciting to move with a duffle bag and nothing else. She said she wasn't scared because she knew we'd take care of them, but she felt odd moving to a place she'd never seen while her friends returned to their homes that night. We planned to move back home by Thanksgiving or Christmas at the latest, so moving felt like an adventure. After weeks of a hard gallop, we arrived at the bed and breakfast Saturday evening with a strong desire for a long, hot bath and a blissful sleep in a clean bed.

We evacuated just four weeks after the big rain.

5

HEAVENLY BED AND BREAKFAST

It was dusk as we drove along the tree-lined circular driveway and parked in front of a three-story plantation-style house. I gasped as I looked up at the house; it was more beautiful than I'd hoped. The kids couldn't stop grinning as they climbed the wide concrete steps, then gathered on the deep covered porch. Huge potted ferns anchored either side of the antique front door, and a wooden porch swing swayed gently in the breeze. White wicker furniture was grouped on area rugs spaced along the lightly stained wood plank porch. I imagined Shelby reading on that swing, or the five of us relaxing on the comfy couches. I imagined working while the kids did homework on the porch. I was stunned by how beautiful and peaceful it was. I couldn't wait to sip morning coffee on this porch after sleeping late for several days.

An attractive fifty-something woman opened the door. Wearing jeans and boots, with an untucked white tailored shirt, she smiled and walked out to greet us. Wayne introduced us to Kim, and I thanked her for letting us stay.

Kim grinned. "This will work great for both of us. Do you want a tour?"

We nodded, then followed her across the dark oak plank floor in the living and dining rooms. A large antique oak table sat at the center of the dining room. Tall, lace-covered windows lined the outside wall. Kim led us to a huge commercial kitchen, pointed out "our" refrigerator shelves, and invited me to use the kitchen as my own.

"It will be wonderful to cook again!" I gushed as Wayne and the kids grinned. We were tired of alternating between Sonic, Subway, and Pizza Hut.

We returned to the entryway, where Christine grabbed my arm and pointed to our right. "Mom, that beautiful winding staircase is just like the movies! I *love* old houses!"

While pleased at Christine's excitement, I worried how Justin would handle stairs with crutches. I didn't want to call attention to his plight, but I asked if he needed help when I noticed him watching Kim climb the stairs.

A realist, Justin shrugged off my comment and grabbed the curved banister with his right hand. "Thanks, but I have to climb stairs by myself eventually, so I might as well start now. Right?" He moved both crutches to his left hand, faced the stairs, and hopped up on one foot as I sighed in relief.

Wayne called up behind Justin, "Good job, buddy!"

I followed him up, relieved one minor hurdle was behind us.

At the top of the stairs were two beautiful bedrooms with a shared bathroom. The girls immediately claimed the four-poster queen bed in the large room on the left. While Christine and Shelby slept together on vacation, they hadn't shared a room since the home remodel. The girls smiled, then simultaneously fell back on their chosen side. My social observation skills had shrunk as my stress grew, but their broad smiles and sparkling eyes looked sincere. Either they were faking, which would do for now, or they were ecstatic, which was even better. In any case, they had a bed and clean air, which counted as a solid win.

I followed Justin to the bedroom across the hall. A surge of relief overcame me as Justin pulled back the curtain and smiled down at his second-floor view of the yard. The shift from yesterday's tension to tonight's luxury was almost too much to take in. Last night four of us slept on the floor of a mold-infested house, but tonight our children, all of us, were safe.

We followed Kim to the front of the house to see the bedroom she'd selected for Wayne and me. It was perfect, with a large sitting area and a private bathroom with a claw foot bathtub. My shoulders relaxed as the enormity of the change finally sunk in. We were safe.

"This is wonderful!" I gushed while anticipating a warm bath. I felt enveloped in luxury, having a clean place to sleep, eat, and live. The fact that it was beautiful was an unbelievable bonus.

Kim pointed at the hole in our bedroom door. "I still have to put door knobs in, so we'll get going on that right away."

"No problem," Wayne said. "We're all family."

Justin pointed at the small stairwell at the end of the hall. "What's upstairs?"

"My bedroom and bathroom are upstairs. Let me show you the laundry room." Kim winked at me. "I hear you have lots of laundry!"

We discussed our laundry situation. Wayne planned to use a rope and pulley to lift our dirty clothes from the driveway to the second-floor balcony. I'd unwrap contaminated clothes on the balcony, then walk two steps and drop them in the washing machine.

Kim laughed off our concerns about mold spores. "You can't hurt this old house. There are plenty of cracks and openings; mold can't find a home here." I cringed at her cavalier attitude; she clearly hadn't heard how quickly mold could take over a home. At the same time, I hoped she was correct. We'd done everything possible to ensure we didn't bring spores with us. Kim agreed that the pulley system was a good idea and that our clothing should stay on the balcony until it was washed.

Kim introduced us to her boyfriend, Russ, an affable, attractive guy in his early fifties. We chatted while the kids scurried to the van to grab their belongings and organize their antique dressers and armoires. The girls popped in to say they didn't have enough hangers, so I added hangers to the shopping list.

That evening, I relaxed in a deliciously hot bath, then dried with a lavender-scented towel. I climbed up on the antique bed, slid my feet under cool, crisp sheets, and relished the odor-free air, knowing our kids were appreciating the same mold-free cocoons down the hall. *We're safe!* I took a deliciously deep breath, my first in weeks, then smiled as I fell asleep.

On Saturday I focused on getting settled in, which meant taking stock and making lists. We needed food, toiletries, and medicine, for starters. I asked everyone to create a list of essentials.

I took a midmorning break to call my mom in Maryland. I hadn't called in weeks because I couldn't bear telling her how bad it had gotten as we crammed into a corner of our mold-infested home.

I described the grounds as I strolled around our new home. "Mom, it's beautiful! The house has deep covered porches all around. It's secluded, way off the road and surrounded by tall pecan trees, ferns, and gorgeous flowers. Everywhere I look, there's another rose garden or sitting area. It's incredible!"

Mom's voice was like a salve. "Oh wonderful, you've landed on your feet already! You've taken lemons and made lemonade!" I was thrilled to finally report encouraging news after an extremely grim month.

I climbed the porch steps, then sunk into a wicker chair. "But I'm a bit worried about the kids. It's a lot for them to go through. We had to leave everything at the house, and they're far from their friends now."

"The kids will be fine. Remember to love and care for them, and they'll adapt." I expected this response, it was Mom's core theme when I voiced concerns about our kids' education, friends, or activities. I trusted her and wanted to believe that children thrived as long as they were loved and cared for, but had trouble believing that was all it took. After the month we had endured, I clung to her words more strongly than before.

I drove to a convenience store for milk early Sunday evening. The bed and breakfast was beautiful, but remote, and I didn't have time to drive to the grocery store in town. On the way back, a pickup truck suddenly appeared in my rearview mirror, then followed me closely. He hugged my bumper, dropped back, then hugged it again. I pulled over to the gravel shoulder some, but he didn't pass. He slowed, then raced back to my bumper, his windshield looming high in my rearview mirror. When I sped up a little, he matched my speed. After repeating this several times the truck roared around me. I told Wayne as soon as I walked in the kitchen, and he asked if I was driving too slow.

"No! Even if I was, he could easily go around me; there's no traffic anywhere around here. That was the only vehicle I saw on the entire trip."

Wayne put the milk on our refrigerator shelf. "That's for sure."

"If anything happens to me, look for a big blue truck. The guy had blond hair and a high forehead but I couldn't see much else." I was stunned. I'd never experienced this before and I certainly didn't expect it on a quiet country road.

Christine and the kids left early for school Monday morning.

Christine dropped Justin and Shelby at the junior high, then circled back to the high school.

On the drive to our house, Wayne and I discussed how to set up our new offices to ensure mold didn't spread beyond our house. We decided to use the six-car detached garage built for our farm equipment, tools, and two vehicles. We'd open the front and back overhead garage doors to force airflow and make it difficult to hold stray spores for long. The garage was new and without leaks, so mold spores couldn't thrive even if they did float in.

We used Clorox Clean-Up to wipe off our office equipment, then created desks out of cardboard boxes. Wayne hooked up the computers and printers, then set up the phone lines. I was relieved to be back at work within a few days. We left the garage door cracked open at night so our cats could come in and out. Since possums and racoons also had access, I cleared notes and files off my cardboard desktop each evening.

I continued calling everyone who knew something about mold. I was desperate for remediation company referrals and information about how to clean moldy items. After many internet searches, conversations, and meetings, I had referrals from multiple sources for several firms specializing in cleaning and rebuilding houses with severe mold problems.

I was upset the insurance company wouldn't provide assistance in our search. I understood they couldn't be involved in our decision; they didn't want to be sued if things didn't work out. But we'd been displaced after a horrible month and had no knowledge about mold or remediation firms. We had no clue which firms were reputable. We didn't know what to look for, what to avoid, or what questions to ask. I was swamped, just trying to get our lives back on track, and now was dealing in unfamiliar territory. This was not an environment conducive to making good decisions, and I had to do lots of research to catch up.

On the plus side, I was skilled at collecting and making decisions based on data. Now that we had a clean place to live and work, I could concentrate on selecting an excellent remediation firm. While the insurance company didn't provide needed information, they covered our claim, which was a huge blessing. I had a lot on my plate, but I could handle it. I was confident we'd be back in our house in a few months.

From a fairly young age, I didn't expect life to be easy or hard. What I did expect was to work and achieve. Work for income, work for fulfillment, work for fun, and work to overcome problems. I remember when my mom dashed my Disney-created dreams during an after-school snack. I'd dismissed her homework question with a new theory floating around first grade—there was no reason for homework because I'd simply get married when I grew up.

"Don't let your grandfather hear you say that!" she snapped as she whirled from the stove to face me. "He's been saving for your college since before you were born. You're going to college, and you will do your homework!"

Stunned, I cautiously nodded.

She softened, then sat next to me at the kitchen table. "Listen, honey, it's fine if you get married and have kids. I'm glad I did." She patted my hand. "But you need a college education first, like me. Things change, and there are no guarantees in life. You need to be able to take care of yourself even if you never marry."

As if my worldview hadn't been altered enough, she added, "There is no prince charming. No one will appear on a white horse and carry you off to a castle. That's not how life works."

I blushed because I still half-believed in the fairy tale.

While part of me was terrified of our mold, I knew that with quality information, effort, and skilled help, we could beat mold. We'd be back home in months with the help of remediators, the insurance company, and my competent husband.

6

NIGHT MOVES

Wayne and I were so exhausted we fell into bed and slept soundly every night. The move, stress, and continuous cleaning of possessions—piled on top of our already busy schedules—resulted in very long days.

Less than a week after our move, my sleep was disturbed by a barrage of lights flashing in sequence across the ceiling and walls. I thought the lights must be from an accident scene on the road, but I didn't hear sirens or noise. My brain couldn't make sense of a soundless light-filled accident at a remote country location. I didn't fully wake, then fell back asleep.

I called to Wayne when I heard water running in the bathroom sink the next morning, "Did you see a bunch of lights flashing on the ceiling last night?"

He walked in slowly, drying his hands on a hand towel. "Yes, I did."

"What was it?"

"I have no idea." He grinned before returning to the bathroom. "But I was too damned tired to get up and look, that's for sure."

The flashing lights appeared again on Friday night, but again I was too exhausted to wake. Late Saturday night, I heard vehicles on the circular drive below our window. I pushed the curtain back, but the front balcony blocked my view of the driveway below. I closed our bedroom door softly behind me and noticed Christine walking down the hall. I quietly asked if she heard anything.

"Yes, it sounded like cars racing on the road," she whispered.

We walked out on the balcony to lean over the railing. The front yard was quiet, the black sky filled with stars. Since there was nothing unusual on the driveway below, we decided to wait. We stretched out on two chaise lounges and chatted in the cool evening air. Forty minutes later headlights appeared and I saw the outline of a truck moving slowly on the road in front of the B&B. The truck paused at our driveway, slowly turned in, then crunched deliberately down the long gravel driveway.

"This is it!" I whispered to Christine excitedly, as Shelby walked out on the balcony.

Christine scooted over to lay in front of me. I propped up a cushion to serve as a last-minute body screen and told Shelby to either hide or go inside. When the truck stopped underneath our balcony, I realized our hiding plan was incomplete; our feet and foreheads remained exposed. I was filled with a sense of dread. *What will we do if they get out of the truck?* I didn't think they'd have the nerve to come down the driveway, and I never imagined they'd park in front of the house.

The truck engine turned off, another thing I didn't expect. Several truck doors squeaked open and clicked closed. My dread intensified as I realized we should go inside but couldn't move without being seen. A few seconds later we heard a loud click, and a blinding light flooded the balcony. I froze while my brain silently screamed, *This is so dangerous; I know they can see us!*

Who let me be a mom and put my daughters in danger? We didn't hear a sound, but the spotlight slowly trailed the length of the balcony. I wondered if they spotted us and were relying on hand signals so we couldn't hear them.

After a ridiculous amount of time that was probably less than three minutes, the spotlight clicked off. Truck doors creaked closed and the engine turned on. I peeked from behind the cushion in time to see the truck roll down the driveway, turn right, then gain speed on the main road.

We scurried inside and locked the door behind us. We embraced in a three-way hug, then raced to our beds.

The next morning, I stopped halfway down the stairs to make sense of the altered living-room scene. Kim sat on a tall kitchen stool stationed next to the partially open front door. Her hand clutched a tattered robe closed at her chin and her bare feet were posted on the stool's lowest rungs. She was engaged in conversation with a tall, beige-uniformed Sheriff's deputy. When Kim heard me, she glanced up with swollen red eyes; clearly she had been crying. I didn't want to pry, and was temporarily distracted by the deputy's cowboy hat, shiny badge, and belt supporting a ridiculous amount of equipment, but would not retreat without answers. Not wanting to directly intrude, I asked Kim if she'd seen Wayne, even though I knew he'd left early that morning.

"He's gone," she responded flatly. She took a long, deep breath and examined me. "I guess I have to tell you. Wayne found a dead deer on Christine's car this morning."

I drew in my breath, then blurted, "A dead deer? What do you mean?"

"Someone killed a deer and left it on the hood of Christine's car. Not the full deer, the hind quarters are gone." She paused. "The deer isn't there anymore. Wayne got Russ up, then they called the Sheriff's Department. Russ and the deputy put the deer in the bayou, so it's gone now. Wayne said he was late for a church vestry meeting, but he'd be back by 9:30 to catch you up."

I blinked furiously to process the wild story. It was Sunday morning; I was thinking of waffles, church, and a lazy day before school started Monday. Instead, this remote zip code presented us with dead deer on car hoods. I didn't question Wayne's attending the meeting, since he did what he could before leaving to honor his commitment. I assumed it was like a continuation of the prior month for him; just doing what had to be done—but the hits just kept coming. I knew he'd fill me in later. What really bothered me was why was a dead deer, I mean the front portion of a dead deer, on the hood of our daughter's car?

I dove in since my story felt exceptionally relevant, "Christine, Shelby, and I saw a truck drive up to the house last night."

The deputy's belt gear jingled as he ambled over and opened a notepad. "Can you describe the truck?"

"It was dark, so I couldn't see the color. But it had an extra-long, low bed and a small cab; it was an unusually shaped truck." I relayed the frightening balcony spotlight incident to them as well.

As I described the truck's long, low bed, I noticed Kim and the deputy exchanging knowing glances. After the deputy finished questioning me, Kim pulled me to the living room and said, "There's something I need to tell you."

Kim filled me in on her domestic situation, which apparently was now *our* domestic situation. Her grown sons were doing everything they could to ensure her fledgling bed and breakfast business failed.

"When you described the truck, we knew whose truck it is. It's Jed's, my youngest," Kim told me. "He and his brother Ralph are still angry with me for divorcing their father. I think they've broken things around here and stolen tools, but I can't prove it's them. They want my business to fail."

I struggled to make room for the flood of new information. *Is she saying what I think she's saying?*

Kim glanced side to side. "They even shot out some of the second-floor windows."

"What?" I exploded. "They shot out windows? You have *got* to be kidding me! Why didn't you tell us?"

Kim gazed down at her pink toenails. "I didn't want to scare you."

"Don't you think we *should* be scared?" I clenched and released my fists. I couldn't believe what I was hearing.

"Nobody was living here then. I don't think they'd do it now that you live here."

"You don't know that for sure. Is one of them blond with a high forehead?" I demanded.

She nodded slowly, wide-eyed.

"Well, he tried to run me off the road our first day here." I swerved to my primary concern, our kids. "Christine drives the kids to school every morning and she comes home late at night. How can we keep our kids safe?"

Kim pleaded with me. "They won't hurt you guys. They just want you to move out so my business will fail."

Backed into a corner, I lashed out, "We *can't* move out! Why doesn't anyone get it?" I was furious. "We can't move out. We have *no place to go!*"

I walked upstairs, shaking my head in disbelief while trying to calm down. The driving intimidation and the dead deer had their intended effect: I was scared—hair raised up on the back of my neck, scared. But we couldn't leave because, as toxic-mold refugees, we had absolutely no place to go. Protecting our kids just became more difficult. I yelled for the kids to come out to the hallway landing.

"Listen. If I come to your room or yell 'Get on the floor,' do it right away. Don't ask questions; just do it! Do you understand?" Backs erect against the wall, their stunned faces nodded in silent unison. I rarely yelled. I could be stern, and actions had consequences. Like Wayne, I could talk any issue to death, but yelling was not mine or Wayne's go-to option.

I stopped pacing to focus my full attention on who was uncharacteristically silent. "Especially you, Shelby! Don't ask why or say something smart; just DO IT! 'Get down' means just that. Get down on the floor without arguing!"

Wide eyes tracked as I stomped back and forth across the landing. My mind was spinning. We'd finally evacuated to safety, only to discover it wasn't safe. Totally without warning, we'd been targeted. I was furious that instead of rest and recovery, our children were facing gunfire drills. I'd just caught my breath during our escape, only to have the rug pulled out from under me. I shook my head, struggling to decide what else to share with the kids. I didn't want to worry them, but needed to keep them safe. I felt pressured to act quickly to keep up with our changing circumstances.

"And if you hear gunfire, if someone is shooting at the house, get down on the floor, crawl to the closet, and stay down on the closet floor. Got it?" Openmouthed, they nodded, then scooted back to their rooms.

I was livid that our safe haven wasn't safe at all. While we could breathe the air, now I was forced to instruct my kids to duck and cover on demand. I wanted to focus on healing and recovery, not institute military lineups.

Later that afternoon I apologized to each of them, adding it was unlikely anything would happen at the house. I sat next to Justin on his bed, then explained that Kim's sons were angry because she had clients for her new business.

Justin turned toward me, "Why do they want her business to fail?"

"Well, they are mad because she divorced their father."

Justin frowned. "But that still doesn't make sense. The divorce is over, so whatever they do to us won't change anything."

"I agree, Justin. The police are following up, so it's unlikely anything else will happen. Sorry I was upset, but I needed to warn you guys."

I asked Christine to meet me on the porch swing. As we swung, I reassured her that the police were involved, then described Kim's son's aggressive road behavior.

I added, "It's unlikely, but I need you to know that someone might try to bother you while driving. Also, you'll take Dad's cell phone when you drive home late, so you can call us." The conversation pained me. I was angry that I had to add to her worries, but felt she had to be warned.

Thankfully, no incidents occurred over the next several nights or the following weekend, so we settled into a cautious but semi-comfortable routine. We returned our energy to fixing our home. After all, the sooner we returned home, the better for all of us.

Justin and Shelby rode the bus to our moldy house after school. They hung out and did homework in our detached garage office for a few hours, then we drove to the bed and breakfast for dinner and evening activities. Christine arrived later.

Our evenings at the bed and breakfast were pleasant. We took baths, did laundry, ate home-cooked meals, and got ready for the next day. Sometimes we worked and did homework at the dining room table, but usually worked from our beds. Funny how I'd always pushed the kids to work from a desk or the dining table at home because studying in bed was hard on their backs and eyes. It was surprisingly easy to relax my usual rules during this time; they could do homework wherever they wanted as long as they did it. Hell, I didn't care if they climbed under the bed to do homework. All of us were adapting and doing the best we could, and that was all I wanted.

I didn't realize how much we longed for fun and normalcy until I saw how enthusiastically we grabbed for it. I spotted a brown and white stuffed dog on a grocery store shelf. He was chubby and ham-shaped with ridiculously short legs that couldn't possibly prop his gigantic belly off the ground. I impulsively added him to the basket and he became a welcome addition to our second-floor home. The girls randomly named him "Adam" after a favorite cousin they missed. We wondered aloud how Adam spent time in the beautiful big house while we were gone all day, and looked forward to seeing him each evening. After unlocking the front door, Wayne called up the stairs to warn Adam to wipe the chocolate muffin off his face and brush Dorito dust off the bedspread. As the girls giggled, Wayne grabbed the banister and slowly ascended while loudly warning that we were coming upstairs and didn't want to catch him sneak-eating. The girls rushed past their dad to their room, then asked Adam if he had been trying on outfits that didn't make him look fat, because, well, he was fat, and no outfit would hide it.

A month after the dead deer episode, I answered the phone in my garage office.

"Mrs. Milberger, this is Richard Davis, Assistant Sheriff of Southturn County. I have some questions about the incident that occurred at the bed and breakfast where you are staying."

"Oh, wow. I appreciate the call, but I've already given interviews to two of your deputies. With those conversations I'm certain we've covered everything I know." I was pleased the case was finally getting high-level attention because we hadn't heard anything after the initial flurry of interactions. I didn't want to waste the Assistant Sheriff's time since I assumed he was a busy guy.

"Well, if you don't mind I'd like to hear what you saw. It's important."

"Okay. Sure." I repeated my description of the flashing lights, the truck, the spotlight on the balcony, and Wayne discovering the dead deer on the hood of Christine's car.

"Did you see anybody? How many people were in the truck?" He fired his questions off immediately, almost before I finished speaking.

"I didn't see anybody. It was dark and we were hiding behind cushions. I know there was one person, probably two, because the doors slammed more than once when they left. There might have been three door slams."

"What happened next?"

"A Deputy Sheriff came out Sunday morning to interview us. The deputy and Russ got a boat and retrieved the deer from the bayou. They contacted the Game Warden since the deer was killed out of season. The deputy went to Kim's son's house to interview him."

"What happened then?" he asked quickly. I was beginning to wonder if he read the interview transcripts. I'd answered all these questions twice before. He didn't appear to be taking notes, because he didn't pause between questions. As I answered, I became slightly irritated at repeating myself a third time. I had other things to do. I needed to work and I had a moldy house to fix.

I continued, "When Kim's son came to the front door the Deputy asked him who was driving his truck the night before. Kim's son said, 'I don't know who was driving, I was too drunk to remember!'"

I giggled in spite of myself, then continued. "I can't even believe it's okay to tell a police officer, 'I was too drunk to know who was driving my truck!' They didn't even bother cleaning the truck. When the Deputy checked, he found blood on the truck bed. He sent a blood sample to the lab to see if it matches the blood from the deer on Christine's car."

"That's right. Those results will take a while. Was there anything else you noticed? You didn't see who was in the truck as they drove away?" The Assistant Sheriff kept pestering me about seeing people I already told him I didn't see.

"No. I have no idea who was in the truck. As I said before, I couldn't see anyone." I couldn't figure out why he insisted on asking questions I'd answered before, so I decided to steer the conversation to my agenda, our safety. "Listen, I'm really concerned for my kids. My daughter drives them to school every day, and drives home alone after activities. Sometimes she's on the road late at night." I paused. "You guys need to find out who was involved and arrest them before something else happens."

"We will. But first we have to see if the lab tests prove that deer was in his truck. The samples were sent to a lab out near Waco, so results will take a while. If you think of anything else, give me a call."

I hung up, then found Wayne in the backyard wiping Clorox spray off a metal file cabinet. "Hey, I just got off the phone with the Assistant Sheriff of Southturn County. He asked me a ton of questions."

Wayne glanced up as he tossed the used paper towel into the trash. "That's good news, right?"

"At first I was pleased because I thought the case was getting some attention. Then it got weird. It's like he wasn't even writing down what I said, but asked questions I'd already answered. I don't know what's going on but I'm not going to talk to him again." I paused. "This whole thing is strange, like he has a different agenda, one I don't know about."

Wayne said that it sounded like the right decision to not talk again, then turned the file cabinet over to spray the cabinet base.

That afternoon, Shelby ran from the bus to tell me her teacher demanded we return a library book that had been left in her bedroom. Shelby told the teacher everything in the house was contaminated with toxic mold and no one could go inside except her dad, who had to put on a Tyvek suit and mask first. This teacher was a notorious bully, so we weren't surprised when Shelby puffed out her chest and parroted back the teacher's response, "Well then, you just tell your daddy he better put that spacesuit on, go back in that house, and you bring that book back to the school library where it belongs!"

Wayne and I discussed options. We didn't want to return the book because we thought it could possibly contaminate the library. On the other hand, we knew some people felt we over-reacted to mold. Comments like "Mold is everywhere, just learn to live with it" didn't help. Clearly, this teacher didn't take mold seriously. After giving it more consideration than her teacher, we decided to clean the book so Shelby could return it. Without expert information, and with so many competing views about mold's impact, it was tough navigating the correct plan of action. In 2002, we couldn't check Google or ask knowledgeable friends. There was no body of available data and we didn't know anyone else facing these decisions. The only source of information was our insurance company, and they offered little guidance. I was frustrated at the lack of assistance about how to clean items, and we struggled to do the right thing based on our research. This responsibility, and the loneliness of our situation, wore on us terribly.

To prepare, Wayne created a list of what he needed from the house. He knew he'd forget everything once he got inside. Wayne had an incredible memory, so writing a list before entering the house was a frightening reminder of how dangerous our mold was. In the past, it wasn't enough for Wayne to say something could be found "in the garage." Instead, he instructed me to "turn right at the door, walk to the third set of shelves, and look on the top left shelf, about shoulder-height in a clear plastic shelving unit."

Not now. Now he had to write a list to remember a few items.

Wayne zipped the white Tyvek suit and pulled the hood tightly. After adding the facemask, all that was left were blue eyes and smile lines. He returned with the necessary items and complaints about how awful it was inside our house. He and I wiped the items off and left them in the sun to kill possible remaining mold spores. Shelby returned the sunbaked library book to her teacher.

In late October we were assigned a new adjuster, Ronnie. Unfortunately, Ronnie was too busy to meet or even talk for an additional week. We were close to selecting a remediation firm, but the firm couldn't do anything without test results and a corresponding remediation plan. We didn't have the test results report or a remediation plan. It was disappointing to lose days, and devastating to lose an entire week. Clearly, we wouldn't be home by Thanksgiving.

I contacted our favorite remediation firm, CleanHome, to ask if anything could be done about our art collection. We treasured our collection of signed prints and watercolors we'd purchased over the years. I worried they wouldn't survive our humid, toxic home. I clutched the receiver close and pleaded, "It is really humid where we live. Without air-conditioning to pull down the moisture, the mold is getting worse. I'm worried our artwork will be ruined."

"I'm sorry, ma'am, but our hands are tied until we get the remediation plan. Once we get it, we can move quickly." I was grateful for the reassurance of a future quick response, but the reality was that nothing was being done to safeguard our house or our possessions.

I spent much of the next week prodding Ronnie and the testing firm. I finally called Bart, Ronnie's supervisor, and spelled out my concerns. "Ronnie is dragging his feet and we aren't making any progress. He doesn't have time to meet with us and it's been weeks since our house was tested. The house is closed up and with our high humidity the mold grows every day."

I paused and then continued, "We're expected to take action to minimize damage, but we can't get anyone to clean our house without a report. How can we minimize damage if nothing is being done to protect our house and possessions? We need that testing report to start the process."

Bart told me he'd get answers and call back. He was cooler when he called the next day. He said he reviewed our concerns with his manager, and Ronnie would call and would get the report to us.

I responded, "OK. I'll call Ronnie in the morning."

"No. Ronnie will call *you*," Bart replied firmly.

Hmm, I thought, there's no need to get short with me, Mr. Insurance Adjuster Manager. I imagined he wasn't sitting at a cardboard box desk in a garage outside a house with toxic mold. I imagined he had air-conditioning. I guessed he didn't have cats, raccoons, or possums sleeping on his desk at night. His desk was in a locked office, not a garage with the overhead door cracked open. He'd enjoy Thanksgiving dinner in his clean home with non-Jell-O air. I didn't think he should be snippy when I pushed for progress. I thought he should be more understanding, and help move the process forward from his clean air-conditioned office.

I didn't voice those thoughts to Ronnie's manager when they jumped to the front of my brain. I shoved them back. Voicing such thoughts wouldn't help our situation at all. I've always held my own in most verbal disagreements and was sometimes harsh under the stress of sixteen-hour days. It took years to realize it wasn't okay to shed stress like beads at a Mardi Gras parade. It wasn't attractive, appreciated, or productive. I worked to develop effective coping skills, and my top three were exercise, work, and rum. While I sometimes failed, this wasn't one of those times.

That week our usual UPS driver pulled into the parking area in front of the garage. I got up from my desk while truck fumes and noise flowed into my office via the cats' partially open garage door. The driver knocked on the back door of the house and was again surprised when I opened the garage door a few feet behind her. I'd explained our situation but it never seemed to sink in; she always approached the house instead of the garage, probably because our house looked normal outside. I thanked her as my garage office phone rang, then closed the door and rushed to answer the phone. Unfortunately, the truck idled outside, filling my space with exhaust fumes and engine noise while I struggled with my phone conversation. I hoped she'd leave, then finally realized she was either completing paperwork or eating lunch. I put down the receiver and walked out to wave the startled driver away. I felt bad, but I couldn't hold a phone conversation with the vapor and racket.

While the garage office was functional, we needed restroom facilities outside our contaminated house. Wayne's next project was to create a bathroom in the back corner of the garage. Luckily, he'd planned for the possibility of a garage bathroom, so the plumbing, including a shower drain, was built in the slab. He installed a toilet and sink over the next few days. He positioned two huge metal shelves full of tools to serve as makeshift walls, then hung a shower curtain as a door. The resulting restroom area wasn't totally private, but it semi-shielded the area from the rest of the garage. It was wonderful not to have to use the restroom in the house, holding my breath all the while.

We moved the washer and dryer to the yard, then sprayed and wiped the inside and outside with Clorox spray. After drying in the sun, we set them up in the garage. When the weather cooled off, we'd need long-sleeved shirts, jeans, and jackets from inside the house. We decided I'd wash clothing retrieved from our house in the garage laundry. We didn't want to jeopardize the B&B by continuing to hoist moldy clothes to the second-floor laundry.

I was thrilled when Wayne upgraded my office space to a shiny white utility trailer. The trailer was small, but there was enough room for a desk, chair, and plenty of files. It didn't have windows, but I didn't need potential leaks or distractions anyway. Wayne attached the electric and phone lines to the side of the house, draped them to the trailer, then poof, I had electricity, air-conditioning, and phone service! He hooked up my computer, printer, and phone, and I was back in business! It was wonderful to have an office door—any door—so I could take calls without interruptions from noisy UPS trucks, and great to secure my workspace from wild and domestic nighttime visitors.

I cooked as often as possible now that I had access to a clean kitchen at the B&B. I made a large pot of vegetable beef soup on Sunday, one of our favorites. I focused on healthy meals that were easy for Christine to warm up when she came home in the evening. It was comforting to have a place to cook healthy meals for my family. Even though we were displaced, I was grateful for the clean kitchen, the pantry space, and the refrigerator shelves.

7

TESTING REPORT

Our new adjuster, Ronnie, finally called to provide a new phone number that should work in three days. He said our testing report was almost ready and we set a meeting for Thursday afternoon. Ronnie's plans changed, so he arrived several hours early. Unfortunately, I was busy on an important conference call. Ronnie and Wayne met without me.

That night I reviewed our testing report and remediation plan. Wayne and I were extremely concerned with the report. Not because we had toxic mold, we already knew that. We were concerned that mold tests weren't conducted in our bedroom, closet, or bathroom vanity. The mold started in the bathroom shower, so it made absolutely no sense not to test the bathroom vanity. The closet was between the tub and the vanity, so it needed to be tested as well. Our bedroom shared a wall with the shower, and that wall definitely needed testing.

The report clarified a critical fact: If tests weren't conducted in an area, then no significant remediation would be done in that area. Remediators would clean every room, but wouldn't remove cabinets or other built-ins unless required based on test results. If no tests were performed, cabinets and vanities wouldn't be removed. If there was mold under our bathroom vanity, it would remain there.

Not testing our bathroom vanity didn't make sense; it was close to ground zero for our mold explosion.

Equally alarming, the plan didn't require testing or cleaning our heating, ventilation, and air-conditioning (HVAC) unit, or the ductwork. Right or wrong, the bathroom exhaust vent was on while we were in the house, as was the air-conditioning. We ran the air-conditioning during the early weeks to lower the humidity and stop mold growth. Spores from the bathroom were definitely in the ductwork and HVAC unit, and were certainly flourishing in our humid attic. It didn't make sense to clean our house and ignore the HVAC system. When the HVAC was turned back on, spores would flow back to the house. This remediation plan wasn't close to adequate.

I called Ronnie to discuss our concerns. "We need every room sampled and every wall. We need the HVAC tested internally. You know there's mold in the unit and the ductwork."

Ronnie quickly retorted, "I don't know anything about mold. You need to talk to the testing firm; that is why we hire experts."

I was thrown back on my heels by Ronnie's reply. If the testing firm didn't do a thorough job of testing and planning the remediation, it's *our* responsibility to check their work? *When did I become an expert in mold remediation? Did my adjuster—my insurance company contact—just say he won't help us navigate the process or offer minimum standards or pointers?* I'd never done mold remediation and it was a steep learning curve, but I knew if they didn't clean the air ducts the house would never be clean. *Shit, shit, shit, this is going to be a wild ride.* I was angry and worried. We were never going to get done at this rate, if no one was accountable for a professional plan of action. I couldn't believe I wouldn't get any guidance. Of course, Ronnie knew more about mold than me; anyone who'd been through this process before or reviewed one mold remediation plan knew more than me.

This illogical remediation plan sent off alarms in my gut. It reminded me of crouching under my desk during Cuban Missile Crisis duck and cover drills. My school was nine miles from the White House, and even at six, I knew desks weren't adequate bomb protection.

Wayne and I agreed that the plan was terribly inadequate and would extend our remediation timeline before we even began. I found Ronnie's reflexive abandonment frightening. It was clear we couldn't count on our adjuster for adequate guidance, support, or even common sense. Any chance of getting our house clean would be due to our efforts, not help from this insurance adjuster.

The next week was a flurry of phone calls to the testing company, the insurance company, potential remediators, and dry cleaners. I decided we had to get our clothing out, cleaned, and stored someplace safe. Luckily, Ronnie agreed, so I contacted numerous dry cleaners. Several cleaners accepted moldy clothing and some even had specific cleaning procedures to deal with mold. I developed an ad-hoc procedure for selecting experts since I couldn't get guidance from Ronnie. I asked each dry cleaner how they processed moldy clothing, and noted their approach in my spiral notebook. The more sensible details I heard, the better. The more confirmation from different sources or vendors, the better. One company ozoned dry clean-only garments for eight hours and then proceeded with the dry-cleaning process. They washed machine-washable items in bleach or a biocide cleaner. Unfortunately, this contact couldn't name the biocide cleaner, which was disappointing since I wanted to wash our retrieved jackets and clothing in the same manner.

I also tried to get information from the testing company, but that was a more difficult process. I remember pressing one contact ("Is washing clothing adequate to remove toxic mold? Does it have to be warm or hot water or is cold okay? Do I need to bleach everything?") The company representative kept offering disclaimers and got frustrated with my insistence on specifics of how to clean things. Finally, she understood I wanted to avoid contaminating the bed and breakfast, and wasn't trying to trip her up or collect information to use against the company. Then she relaxed and provided basic cleaning facts, which I was thrilled to get. This information became my basic list of best practices, which I updated each time I talked to a knowledgeable source.

I called Christopher at CleanHome, our top choice for remediators so far. He agreed our testing plan was inadequate. He said we should push to have more thorough testing done so a comprehensive remediation could be done. Apparently, the three young testers that arrived without personal protective equipment weren't up to the job after all. Those testers were hired by our insurance company.

Christopher added, "If the insurance company refuses to let you have more thorough testing, you can threaten to sue."

"I don't want to start out that way. I'll call the testing company to see what they say."

I called Christy at the testing firm and voiced my concerns about the scope of the testing. I began with questions I had heard would determine whether a testing firm is knowledgeable. "Who does your lab work? Who signs off on the report?"

"We do our own lab work and we have a microbiologist who signs the report." I was surprised that both were the "correct" answers. Then she asked if we had checked our water lines for leaks. I told her we didn't have plumbing leaks, just one small leak due to an extreme rain.

"You don't know that until you do a pressure test. The lines need to be tested to ensure there are no other leaks. There is no point trying to clean your house if you still have leaks; the mold will keep growing," she continued.

"Well, that makes sense," I agreed.

Convinced that her firm knew what they were doing and certainly knew more than me, I asked what else we should do to make sure the process went smoothly. I added my concerns that they hadn't tested our bedroom, closet, or bathroom vanity.

"You can ask us to re-sample or you can hire another company to do so. You should get the plumbing test done. You should definitely get the HVAC system evaluated." She paused, then continued. "Make sure you hire a remediation company that knows what they are doing. Check with the Better Business Bureau to make sure there aren't any claims against them. Mold remediation follows the same practices as asbestos abatement, so keep that in mind." She added, "We are a reputable testing firm. We are hard to pass from; most clients don't pass on their first try."

Convinced that the testing firm was at least well-informed, I took her advice and continued researching CleanHome, our top remediation firm. I got good reviews when I called their competitors, which was excellent news. I got glowing recommendations about Christopher, our contact at CleanHome. A review of CleanHome's BBB report didn't reveal a single complaint. All the information I collected about CleanHome was positive.

After much negotiation, we got verbal agreement from our adjuster for the additional testing we requested.

Unfortunately, Ronnie reneged on his promise the next day.

"I talked with TESTX and the insurance company and they both agree we need to start the remediation. We can't keep testing, we need to start cleaning," Ronnie demanded.

I sighed. The mold was certainly worse with the air-conditioner off and the humidity rising unchecked. The humidity was 75 percent yesterday; our spores were definitely reproducing in that environment. The big rain occurred over two months ago and we hadn't started cleaning the house. I was so frustrated. Waiting was risky because the mold was growing, unchecked. But flawed testing would lead to flawed remediation. Flawed remediation would cost us precious time because we'd have to repeat the testing and remediation process.

I pleaded with Ronnie. "With inadequate testing and remediation, it will take forever to get the house clean. This piecemeal approach of partial testing followed by partial cleaning will drag the process out."

"That's why we better get started," he snapped.

I wasn't impressed with Ronnie's grasp of mold remediation or his interpersonal skills; he was a terrible fit as an insurance adjuster. I could think of other jobs he'd be better suited for, but that wasn't the task for today. I called the testing firm's recommended plumbing company to schedule the plumbing leak check.

I called our insurance agent to request a new adjuster. "Bruce, he'll cost the insurance company more time and money. The testing and remediation plan isn't thorough enough. We know we'll need more testing and accompanying remediation before we start the first remediation. We're already behind before we begin!"

Bruce was helpful as always, saying he'd make some calls and get back to me.

I got off the call as the first few raindrops hit the roof of my utility trailer office. Although I loved my new office, rain was a problem. The trailer was basically a large tin can on wheels. Raindrops sporadically pinging on the tin roof became deafening when the drops increased to a rainstorm, which they almost always did. It rained about one third of the time, so I became adept at ending calls after the first few pings. Unfortunately, I couldn't quickly disengage from the corporate labor attorney one afternoon, and within minutes the drops predictably amplified to a driving rain. I blushed deeply, then turned beet red as the trailer filled with the sound of machine gun fire. It was impossible to hear each other over the din, so I yelled that I'd call him back, then hung up. I felt the heat radiate from my scalp and forehead as I sat in my tiny metal office; I was completely mortified. It was unusual to work from home when I started in 1986, so I strove to ensure my office looked and sounded professional. This became quite difficult as my office condition deteriorated; the most recent reminder was my battle to shield my phone conversation from the UPS truck's rumbling engine. But this was the corporate labor attorney, someone I respected and worked closely with. He knew I was temporarily working from a trailer, but I had hoped my work contacts would quickly forget my office situation. Not in this case; he teased me for weeks about officing from the front lines of Vietnam. From then on, his calls began with comments like "Are you expecting enemy fire this afternoon?" I was glad he was comfortable making light of it, but mortified that it remained clearly fixed in his mind.

Wayne was working on an improved office situation for both of us. He ordered a portable building finished out with two rooms to use as offices. He planned to set the building next to our garage until the house was clean, then later move it to the farm and use it as an office.

Justin rushed off the bus Monday afternoon to ask if we had a dictionary.

"No, it's in the house. What do you need a dictionary for?" I responded.

"We have to write definitions for our spelling words for English and it's due on Wednesday."

I told him not to worry and assured him I'd get a dictionary. But after visiting six stores, none of them (including our local bookstore) had a dictionary. I didn't have time for a two-hour round trip to Walmart, so when Justin got off the bus on Tuesday, I said we'd go to the library.

"Mom, I have to write definitions every week. Will we go to the library every week?" He was obviously concerned with my plan.

"Just until I have time to find a dictionary. It'll be fine. I'll get one." I was frustrated. We had at least four dictionaries, one of them gigantic, in the moldy house.

Wayne and I worked hard to provide for our kids. The idea that Justin didn't have the tools to do a basic homework task was foreign to me. My job was to provide what they needed to grow and learn. I wasn't doing my job and in spite of all our efforts, we really weren't providing for our kids. This hit me hard, and it hurt.

Later that evening I returned the reference dictionary to the librarian while Justin loaded his backpack. The librarian had a son in Shelby's grade. We chatted a bit, then she asked how we were doing.

"Oh, fine," I replied.

Her warm brown eyes drilled into mine. "Everyone knows about your house. We all feel sorry for you guys."

"Thank you," I responded. "We'll be at the library more often for a while. I can't find a dictionary and Justin needs one for homework."

Her tiny frame leaned forward as she slid the dictionary back across the counter to me. "Take it," she whispered loudly.

I tilted away from the counter and protested, "I can't take it. It's a reference book!"

"Take it!" she insisted.

"We aren't even allowed to check out reference books!"

She responded firmly, "There is a pile of dictionaries next to the back door that we don't use. It's all right; just take it."

I realized this matter-of-fact librarian wasn't going to back down. Tears stung my eyes as the kindness of her offer sunk in. Embarrassed, I wiped them away while thanking her multiple times. I clutched the dictionary close so no one saw the title as we walked out.

A deep breath filled my lungs in the clear night air. I relaxed during the drive. "Justin, can you believe she *gave* us a dictionary! Now we don't have to go to the library every week!"

Justin murmured something unintelligible; probably lost in his own thoughts. I was overcome with gratitude at her kind gesture. I've reflected about this many times over the following years. The dictionary gift was a small thing, but it was exactly what I needed. This gesture made me feel that people cared. This gift provided hope that somehow we'd survive this difficult period.

A few days later, the plumbing leak detection specialists arrived on time for their Monday morning appointment. I unlocked the back door for them and headed to my office. Before I could unlock the utility trailer, one of them reappeared on the driveway.

"It really stinks in there!" the younger worker complained.

"Well, yeah; we have toxic mold, so it is going to stink," I responded.

"No, it's *really* bad in there," he replied and turned to walk back in.

I couldn't help shaking my head. What did he expect, roses?

An older guy knocked on my trailer door minutes later. "You have mold growing on your kitchen floor."

Incredulous, I responded quickly, "No I don't." We didn't have visible mold growth. While the house reeked of mildew, our mold was not visible.

"Yes, you do," he hiked his jeans up and planted worn cowboy boots on the pavement.

I wanted to insist again that we did not have mold growing on the kitchen floor, but realized this exchange could continue for some time. Instead, I stepped down from the trailer and offered to get my husband. Wayne left the Clorox Clean-Up bottle on the back porch, put on his mask, and walked in the back door. A few minutes later he returned, shaking his head. "You're not going to believe it, but the refrigerator quit working. Everything in the freezer melted. Defrosted food pushed the freezer door open, then oozed halfway across the kitchen floor."

He sat down on the step and wiped his forehead. "Of course now it has fuzzy black mold growing all over it. It is *totally* disgusting!"

I dropped down beside him. "What now?"

"I guess I need to clean it up. We haven't signed a contract with the remediators, and who knows when they'll actually start. I can't let it grow like that; it will keep getting worse."

After the plumbers left, Wayne put on a mask, rubber gloves, and rubber boots before going inside. Later that afternoon he asked me to come outside.

Wayne stood in the shadow of the garage, holding his rubber gloves. He pulled his mask up on his forehead to talk. "You can't even imagine how disgusting it is in there; it's one of the worst things I've ever seen or smelled. I could barely breathe. It's a huge slippery wet mess of black mold. I used a shovel to load the trash bags, but it kept oozing back off the shovel."

I stepped closer to stand in the shade, and he stepped back, insisting, "Don't get around me; you don't want to breathe this stuff. I've got diarrhea again even though I wore gloves. It's really bad."

Wayne took another step away, then slowly lowered to the grass. "Those bags were so heavy! I partially filled about twenty bags with muck. I couldn't fill them completely because they'd be too heavy to lift. I'm bone tired."

"I'm so sorry," I interjected.

Wayne wiped his brow with the back of his hand. "It was overwhelming. I could barely breathe in there, even though I put a fan in the back doorway to circulate clean air."

After resting a few minutes, he slowly stood. "Now I need to move the refrigerator out."

"By yourself? You can't do that!"

"Well, I can't leave it in there. It has mold growing in it, so it's making it worse in there. I have to do this so our house can begin to get better."

"Do you want me to help?" I asked.

"No," he frowned. "It's terrible in there; I can barely breathe even with the fan on. You definitely don't want to go in. I can move the refrigerator. I just need to get it to the back porch, then I'll hose it out."

He returned to the house and I returned to the office. I'd known about Wayne's tenacity since early in our marriage, but now that our health and home were at risk, his grit was displayed on a bigger scale. While toxic mold was proving to be a huge test of our resilience, and our marriage, I knew I could count on Wayne, on both of us, to do whatever needed to be done.

Frightened at the pace the house was deteriorating, I called Ronnie to see if we could start over and work together as a team. After all, we both wanted the house fixed quickly. We couldn't waste any more time. Even an incomplete remediation was better than no remediation. Ronnie agreed that we should move forward with the current remediation plan. I told him the plumbers completed the leak test and would email their report.

On the way to dance class, Shelby peppered me with questions about the dead deer on Christine's car. Her questions flew over my shoulder while she changed in the back seat.

"What kind of deer was it?" she called while lying on the seat to pull pink tights over her feet and legs.

"What do you mean?"

"Well, was it a mother, a father, or a baby?"

"I don't know; it was just a deer." I was pretty comfortable talking about the situation with the kids now. The deer episode was months ago. We hadn't had more trouble, so it looked like this problem was resolved. Wayne heard the young men wouldn't bother us again because they could get charged with poaching if the blood tests revealed they killed a deer out of season. He said they'd face fines and jail time, so were likely trying to stay out of trouble.

Shelby's French braid flipped from side to side as she pulled her leotard over each shoulder. In an exasperated tone she demanded, "*Mom*, you have to find out. It really matters."

She waited to make eye contact in the rearview mirror before providing needed context. "Christine's car is white, that's a symbol of purity." She let this sink in, then continued. "The hood of a car is like an altar." Her words came faster and with more intensity, "A deer is an innocent and defenseless animal. If it's a mother, or baby, even more so." Shelby leaned close to the front seat to urgently add, "You *have* to find out so we can understand what message they are trying to send us! We need to know if the message is for you, or Dad, or one of us!"

I glanced in the rearview mirror and tried not to smile too broadly at her enthusiasm. "Oh, sweetie, don't worry. I don't think these guys read that much!"

MOLD COACHING

That evening, I sat in the middle of our bed with our test results, the remediation report, my spiral notebook, pens, and my phone arranged in an arc around me.

Wayne stopped to ask what I was doing. I said I was preparing for a 7:15 phone call with Greg.

"Who's Greg?" he asked.

"He is a friend of Gloria's; remember I went to graduate school with her? He lives in Houston and has toxic mold. He knows a lot and is willing to answer my questions." I glanced at the materials arranged in piles, then sheepishly back at Wayne. "He's kind of particular. He wanted the time set exactly, saying he could only spend forty-five minutes with me. He wanted my questions and test results ready for the call. I guess his game, his rules."

Wayne grinned at my arrangement. "Looks like fun."

I reviewed my questions until 7:14, then dialed and introduced myself.

Greg jumped right in. "Do you have your test results with you?"

"Yes," I answered.

"Great." He paused. "Listen, I know it's kind of weird how

specific I was about my requirements for this call. Life got really crazy with our mold situation, so I've become a bit rigid with how I spend my time. There are way too many demands on me. I agreed to talk with you since you're a friend of Gloria's."

"Thank you," I quickly interjected while he took a breath.

"You're welcome. I want to help people through this mess when possible. If I can help someone early in the process, maybe they can avoid some of the problems we had."

Greg continued. "I guess I should give you a summary of our situation first, then we'll get to your story. I have a Ph.D. in Clinical Psychology. My wife is working on her dissertation, and we have a six-year-old daughter. We've been fighting toxic mold for three years. We had eight remediations and our house still isn't clean. The house is sealed up and we're living in an apartment." Greg paused. "I'm making mortgage payments on a house we can't live in."

"Oh, no!" I exclaimed.

"It's no picnic," he continued. "We sued the remediators and the insurance company, and are working our way through that process."

"Wow. I'm so sorry to hear that."

"Thanks. Let's get to your test results. What types of mold do you have?"

I struggled with the pronunciations. "Penicillium. Chaetomium. Cladosporium. Aspergillus. Stachybotrys. Should I keep going? There are lots more here."

"Wow. Stachybotrys is the really bad stuff. All those you named are serious, so that's all I need to hear."

I reflexively smiled. I guess I figured if I had toxic mold it may as well be the really bad stuff. I was immediately embarrassed by my response, then asked why Stachybotrys was a really bad mold.

"One reason is because even the dead spores are toxic. So

you'll suffer the same negative effects after the mold spores are dead. Aspergillus toxins cause diarrhea. Chaetomium is really bad. It inhibits cell replication. It causes neurological damage, and so does Stachybotrys."

My back straightened as I dropped the pen. *Stachybotrys and Chaetomium cause neurological damage! No wonder Wayne couldn't count the irrigation fittings. No wonder I couldn't think in my office.* I told Greg I couldn't breathe in our bedroom just days after the mold explosion.

"That's right. Severe mold exposure can lead to Dyspnea, often referred to as 'air hunger.' That is when you struggle to get enough air to breathe."

I scribbled as he described the effects of our various molds. He told me to be diligent in taking care of our health and our family because we were entering an extremely stressful period of our lives. He said the entire family should eat well, get plenty of rest, avoid stress when possible, and be kind to each other. I worked through my questions and before I knew it my time was almost up.

Greg said, "Listen. I want you to get ready; you guys are in for a wild ride. It will be really hard on you *and* your family. Your life will be difficult and lonely because people don't understand mold and its impact. Some will dismiss you as crazy. They have no idea how severely toxic mold can impact your health. They have no idea what toxic mold exposure is like and no idea how hard it is to get rid of it."

"Exactly! People say it's all in our mind, that mold is everywhere and we just need to get over it." I paused. "Even our pediatrician told me we 'need to learn to live with mold since it's everywhere.' I went to another pediatrician and he said the same thing!'"

Greg exhaled. "Yeah, it's tough to battle misinformation in addition to everything else. But believe me, toxic mold is real, it's dangerous, and it is very tough to eradicate." Greg sighed. "My wife is having a difficult time. I said she's working on her dissertation." He paused, and his voice caught when he continued, "But I don't think she does much of anything except take care of our daughter. I'm pretty sure she's depressed. It can be overwhelming."

"I'm so sorry."

"Yeah, it's rough, but we're lucky because we can afford to get away from it. Not everyone is so lucky. Oh, that's another thing. Your insurance money is yours. Don't sign it over to the remediators. I've heard of remediators doing a partial job, then leaving a widow sitting on a folding chair in a shell of a house. There are terrible crooks in this business who will take your last dime and not look back. Do your homework."

"I will," I promised.

"I need to get going. Remember to take care of yourselves. Your lives will never be the same again. I can answer additional questions, so call me in a few months to let me know how it's going."

My mind raced as I summarized our meeting notes. I was ecstatic to finally have someone explain our test results, answer questions, and provide a preview of what to expect. Now I knew why Wayne got diarrhea after cleaning the shower area; Aspergillus toxins cause diarrhea.

I had trouble grasping that the wild ride was just beginning; surely our ride began with the toxic mold explosion. Surely things would get better once we got our possessions cleaned and stored in a safe location. Things would definitely improve when they started cleaning our house. Certainly my extensive vetting of remediation firms meant our situation would be different, and we'd return to a clean house after two or three remediations, tops.

I couldn't fathom how his house was still contaminated after three years and eight remediations. He was intelligent, well-informed, and organized, so the fault didn't appear to lie with him. I was determined to use this information to avoid the same pitfalls, but couldn't grasp how, after eight remediations, his house still wasn't clean.

The next few weeks were a flurry of work, kids' activities, and trying to live a normal life despite our circumstances. After a long day of meetings in Houston, I walked across the B&B's dark porch and opened the front door to Janice Joplin singing "Oh Lord, won't you buy me a Mercedes Benz?" I smiled and followed her pleading lyrics to the living room.

"That's my favorite song!" I told Kim as the weight of the day and the eighty-mile drive fell from my shoulders.

"Wayne told me! It's mine as well!" Kim grinned.

Wayne was beaming. He knew I'd be thrilled to hear Janice's raspy voice and plaintive lyrics. Janice knew more than her share about suffering. She always put a smile on my face. While our house had toxic mold, we were, at this moment, in a beautiful, clean house listening to Janice.

November brought cooler, dark mornings, and, unfortunately, a pair of still-exhausted parents. When Christine insisted we come downstairs one morning because there was something weird in the kitchen, well, I hate to admit that we didn't. She mentioned early-morning kitchen noises several times, with Shelby confirming she heard noises and the kitchen was creepy. Wayne and I were so exhausted we told them to eat then go to school.

Early the next morning Christine planted herself next to our bed, her hands balled into fists at her side. "Mom, Dad! You *have* to come downstairs now! Something is coming up from under the floor! It pushed the metal vents up off the floor."

We flew down the stairs to find several brass heating registers in various states of disarray along the hallway. One register was pushed up entirely onto the floor, leaving a dark rectangular hole gaping open. Without coffee or context, I was clueless. *What could cause this? Aliens? Really big roaches? Nothing has ever arisen from beneath the floor of my house, how about you?*

Wayne didn't need additional information. Visibly irritated, he nudged one of the registers with his toe, "Why in the hell aren't the screws tightened? How did raccoons access this ductwork? It's supposed to be a closed system."

I flicked on all the lights while imagining hungry wild animals trying to join our children for Cheerios. Wayne ensured that all the registers were secure by that evening, and the raccoons never resurfaced. *Damn it, things could have been much worse; my kids were barefoot in that dark hallway.*

When we lived in our house, one of Shelby's coping mechanisms had been to unleash on our black lacquer upright piano after a tough day at school. She'd rush off the bus, head straight for the den, and play until the music calmed her. Junior high presented plenty of drama and she clearly missed this outlet, so Wayne and I surprised her with an electric keyboard on her birthday. She was excited, but she couldn't hide her disappointment at its tinny sound. It didn't compare to the Yamaha's rich tones, but would have to suffice until we moved home. We were doing the best we could, but mold didn't make us tone-deaf, and an electric keyboard was not the same as a real piano.

I was thrilled when we finally got a new adjuster—we wouldn't have to deal with underachieving Ronnie anymore. An insurance adjuster who declared he didn't know anything about mold; what a prince.

We discussed our clothing during my first phone call with Kevin, our new adjuster. I had been sorting and washing clothes that we needed and throwing away clothes we didn't need. I knew what dry cleaners charged and I didn't think our old, or outgrown, clothes were worth the cleaning price. Kevin's answer was clear. "I don't have a problem with dry-cleaning costs. If you want it, get it cleaned, it's that simple. Keep the invoice and I'll reimburse you." It was wonderful to get clear guidance on the rules of the game.

I continued researching dry cleaners until I found one that sounded like they could handle our job. When I asked how they cleaned moldy clothes, the dry cleaner said they followed the normal dry-cleaning process but didn't reuse the solvent. When I asked how they cleaned leather items like shoes or purses, she replied, "We spray them with biocide, then treat them with ozone for at least ten minutes. Then we wipe the items down and rub them with Saddle Soap so they are preserved and stay soft."

"We have a lot of stuff and it's in pretty bad shape. I mean, our clothing really smells terrible. Are you sure you can handle items with toxic mold?" I asked.

"Oh yes ma'am, we deal with mold items often. Just bring it in."

The following Monday, Wayne and I packed the back of my van with black trash bags. Each bag contained moldy clothes, tightly tied, placed inside yet another trash bag facing the opposite direction, and tied securely again. We only took clothing needed for the next few months since the dry cleaner would pick up the rest in a few weeks. We didn't need linens, comforters, and sleeping bags while we lived in the B&B. I wouldn't need baby clothes or christening outfits until we had grandchildren.

Once on the road, I suggested we expand our outing to include lunch at a cool restaurant. My lunch-date excitement faded when Wayne announced the van smelled bad. The wet-socks odor had escaped the bags to surround us. I was shocked when I realized double-bagging the clothes wasn't adequate.

Minutes later, Wayne confessed he felt light-headed and needed his window open. As his window whirred down, I said, "Open all of them. I feel spacy too."

Wayne repeatedly looked down to fumble with the levers, then finally succeeded in lowering the remaining windows.

His chest leaned forward, and his chin jutted out past the steering wheel.

He squinted at the windshield like he was negotiating a dense fog. But the sun was out and there was no fog.

Alarmed, I sat up straight. "Wayne, are you okay?"

As he deliberately turned to respond, the car veered slightly right.

He immediately slowed and righted the car. He pushed his eyes closer to the windshield, and flatly responded, "No. I'm not."

This was not normal behavior. Wayne was a comfortable, experienced driver, able to handle poor visibility along with a backseat full of distractions. He had used complex instruments and multiple data sources when acquiring a commercial pilot's license; he didn't fumble with window levers or veer off the road while chatting. Now he drove like a drunk. But he wasn't drunk.

The right front tire hit gravel the next time he tried to speak. Again, he slowed down to steer back to the pavement.

His jaw tightened while his eyes remained glued to the road. "Listen, I won't be able to drive if it gets worse. I feel like I've been drugged. I can't function."

His words slowly floated in a white cartoon bubble until they hung suspended over my head, waiting for my dull brain to comprehend. I knew *I* couldn't drive. I doubted I could unhook my seatbelt without assistance.

We were in trouble. Part of me recognized I should panic, but I didn't have the mental capacity to panic. My reaction time was diminished. Every thought and action dragged out in slow motion.

I was terrified, except I was too stupid to panic and too slow to react.

We focused our remaining cognitive ability on getting to safety. Wayne inched the car along the asphalt at a pace he could manage. I leaned out of the window, yelling and pointing at road signs as cattle munched grass in an adjacent field. Wayne concentrated on safe driving and following my directions.

By the time we arrived at the strip center parking lot we could barely function, even with ventilation from fully open windows. We managed to spot the dry cleaners across the parking lot, but the medians and curbing were too difficult to navigate. It was pitiful and frustrating; I pointed while he tried negotiating at a snail's pace. After ten minutes of exasperated pointing, corrections, and multiple-point turns, we arrived at the dry cleaners. We exhaled in relief when the van was parked and the ignition off. I leaned my head over to my lap to recover, then jerked back. We couldn't relax until the moldy bags were out.

We unloaded our bags in the waiting area, then paused in the open door to remind the startled employee to treat our items immediately. We sat in the van, dumbfounded, until Wayne finally felt he could safely drive. We located a restaurant, then waited for service in stunned silence. Suddenly, memories burst forward.

"We couldn't drive through a small parking lot without getting lost! We could see where we wanted to go but still couldn't get there!" I couldn't believe how impaired we'd been.

Wayne looked up from his plate, "It's absolutely insane. This stuff is really bad; the military should weaponize it."

I nodded vigorously. "Exactly. We knew the air in our house was horrible. But I didn't imagine that moldy clothing could make me stupid, and *so quickly*. It's terrifying."

Wayne frowned. "We have to be super careful bringing anything to the B&B; we simply cannot contaminate it." He shook his head. "I can't believe how dangerous this mold is. I couldn't drive! I drove a tractor at twelve!"

"No one will believe this. I don't believe it and it just happened to us."

We fell back into our own thoughts on the drive back. I was devastated and frightened by how quickly and dramatically the mold affected our ability to think and perform simple tasks. To this day it still terrifies me.

One minute I was fine.

Fifteen minutes later I couldn't function.

All because of the air we breathed.

A few days later, Wayne asked me to sit down after he returned from the farm. He said a local rancher told him who was in the truck the night the dead deer was left on Christine's car. Until now, we only knew Kim's son was in the truck.

"You'll never guess who else was in the truck. Remember the Assistant Sheriff, the one who called to ask questions you'd already answered?"

I nodded, wide-eyed.

"The Assistant Sheriff's son was in the truck!"

"No way!" I exclaimed. "That's why he kept asking what I saw, because his son was with them? He wasn't trying to help me. He wanted to know if I could identify his son!" Now I understood why the phone call was so weird. "What kind of place is this where the Sheriff Department's strategy is to cover the whole thing up? Is this when people call in the Texas Rangers?"

Wayne grinned as he relaxed back in his chair. "Yeah, but that's probably not necessary. The B&B has been quiet for months now. I'm sure those guys are pretty nervous with the attention this case has gotten. I'm sure nothing else will happen."

"Good. I don't have time for the Texas Rangers anyway. I can barely keep up with the catastrophe we have. We certainly don't need more drama."

By mid-November, I'd done all the checking, internet searches, referrals, and phone interviews I could do. Wayne and I still felt the remediation plan was inadequate, but we had to move forward with cleaning. Christopher at CleanHome had impressed us. He was well-informed and always willing to answer questions. I couldn't find any red flags about him or CleanHome, so we decided to hire them.

Christopher and his boss, Steve, arrived at our garage office wearing matching black polo shirts embroidered with the company logo. Steve was tall and looked like he spent lots of time doing bicep curls. Christopher was also fit, but leaner. They reviewed the final contract with us, then patiently answered our remaining questions.

After reading for a few minutes, Wayne asked, "The contract says our contents will be cleaned thoroughly and then stored in an air-conditioned warehouse."

"Yes, Mr. Milberger," Steve answered. "As you know, air-conditioning is important to keep the humidity down. Mold needs moisture to grow, so it's important to store items in a dry environment."

"Will our possessions be stored along with other people's moldy contents?" Wayne asked.

"Mr. Milberger, everything is cleaned first. Then your possessions are stored in separate rooms from other customers," Steve responded.

"Separate rooms sound wonderful! We certainly don't want to get other people's mold in addition to ours!" I giggled at the absurd thought that our situation could get worse. I asked what would happen if we needed something from storage.

"Mrs. Milberger, we create a thorough inventory during the move-out, what we refer to as the 'packout.' Every item you own is listed on the packout sheet along with where it is stored, including the box number. If you need something, like your sewing machine, look it up on the packout sheet, then let us know and we'll bring it right to you."

Wayne and I nodded. It would be wonderful to bring clean items back to the B&B as we needed them. We'd purchased everything we needed since we moved out. My refrain when the kids asked where things were was "It's in the house," which meant "We don't have it," which meant "We need to buy it." They barely blinked when we said we didn't have what they needed—they were so used to hearing it. Tape, glue, scissors, stapler, Band-Aids, gloves, medicine, shoes, hats, sports equipment, bathing suits, swim flippers, umbrellas, you name it, we didn't have it.

"Christopher, you said paper, electronics, and leather are the hardest items to clean. How will you clean these?" Even though I'd done lots of research, I was still trying to determine the proper protocol for removing mold from items. With remediation experts in front of me, I wanted answers.

"Well, leather items are sent to a dry cleaner that specializes in mold remediation. We treat the electronics ourselves. Of course, we wipe everything down. That's how we handle books and paper."

"You wipe it down?" I interjected. "Do you mean each page? You wipe down *each* page?"

Christopher shifted in his seat. Steve jumped in, "Yes, Mrs. Milberger, we wipe down *every* page."

Wayne and I exchanged glances. No matter how much we wanted to be on board, we had difficulty believing every page of our hundreds of books would be wiped down. I had a wall of file cabinets and a second wall of books. Wayne had loads of files and the kids had a wall of books as well. But we had to move forward. We had to believe they knew what they were doing and trust they would do it.

I couldn't help thinking about cognitive dissonance, when someone's beliefs or values aren't in line with their actions. People can't handle the contradiction, so they struggle to regain internal consistency to get everything back in agreement. Cognitive dissonance is a powerful, well-researched psychological construct, and it worked on us. If our newly hired remediators said they would clean each page, we needed to believe them because we believed they would clean our house. Of course, they'd been in business for years and had a spotless reputation, so they must be doing it right. We swallowed our doubts.

Still in problem-solving mode, I thought that if they had less paper, maybe they *would* wipe down every page. "We have books and paper that can be thrown away to save cleaning and storage. How should we do that?"

"We'll have plenty of 'burn bags' during packout so you can put items in there that you want destroyed," Christopher answered.

"There are some things we cannot take and store, so you have to remove those items. We can't take valuable items, like guns or jewelry," Steve added.

"Anything else you can't take?" Wayne asked.

"We can't take your piano. A piano company will need to clean it. After we sign the contract, we'll get a company out here to pick it up," Steve replied.

Shelby's beautiful black lacquer upright would be missed. Except she couldn't come in the house to play anyway, so the sooner it was cleaned the better.

I took a deep breath. "I have a lot of very sensitive work material. I'll wipe down and keep some of it with me, but I don't have room for it all. How can I be sure it's safe?"

"Mrs. Milberger, we are entrusted with storing people's lives and everything they own. We take that very seriously. We hire good people and train them well. They know what they're doing and are very trustworthy," Steve answered.

I felt better, but this work material wasn't mine to make decisions about. I decided to review every work item before it was packed. If it was sensitive, I'd clean and keep it or put it in the burn bag for destruction. If no confidential information was stored outside of my possession, then no one would have access to it. I made a note to clear my plan with my employer first.

We signed the contract and shook hands. I was still concerned about the "every page will be wiped down" declaration, but decided not to dwell on it. We had researched and selected a reputable firm. We'd finally signed a contract. Now they could begin cleaning our house!

The afternoon before Thanksgiving, Wayne and I returned to the B&B early. We felt giddy and playful since the contract was signed and cleaning would start soon. I spied Adam, the chubby stuffed dog, on the girls' bed. I put one of the girls' thongs on Adam, then placed him back on their quilt. Wayne and I agreed Adam looked ridiculous in a thong and couldn't wait for Shelby and Christine's reaction. After bounding upstairs, the girls scanned the room, wondering why we sat in their bedroom wearing silly grins.

When their eyes reached the bed, Wayne inquired in a high-pitched voice, "Does this thong make my butt look big?"

"Daad!" Both girls laughed, and for a few minutes life was completely normal.

We had a lovely Thanksgiving dinner at Wayne's brother's house, with tons of food, gorgeous table settings, and lots of hugs and conversation. We were peppered with questions, but everyone was happy to hear about our progress. They were thrilled that remediators would soon empty our house, then begin cleaning.

A few days later Christopher stopped at our house to tell us he'd left CleanHome. He wouldn't provide details and looked uncomfortable with my questions, so I didn't push much.

I didn't want to press, but still asked, "You knew you were leaving when we met last week to sign the contract, right?"

"Yes. He made me go to the meeting since you were my clients and we had a connection. I'm sorry I couldn't tell you." He barely looked at me—it was a painful interaction. He tried to reassure me, "They are a good firm and you guys are in skilled hands. It was just time for me to leave."

I was sad to lose Christopher. We trusted him and he was the reason we signed with CleanHome.

9

PACKOUT

I shoved my tennis shoes into the white Tyvek suit, lifted it to my torso, then wove my arms into both sleeves. I zipped the front, pulled the hood forward over my head, and then tied the drawstring under my chin. I placed the facemask's rubber band under my chin and rested the mask on my head: I didn't need a facemask in the garage. Wayne's hood was pulled so tightly it touched his laugh lines. Clearly, he didn't want spores inside his suit.

We were a mess of mixed emotions. The remediators had scheduled *and* cancelled our packout twice already. Three months after the mold explosion, and still nothing had been done in our house. Cleaning couldn't start until our possessions were removed. We were grateful when two tractor trailer trucks finally arrived with a full crew. However, it was raining very hard, a deluge. So hard that if you stood outside for forty seconds the skin under your clothing would be soaking wet.

I frantically paced the garage. "They can't pack us out in this rain, right?" I worried aloud to Wayne. "Our stuff will be drenched before it gets to the truck. They can't wrap moldy items in blankets, walk them through the rain, then cram them in a truck, right? That's no way to start!"

"I know," he shook his head in disbelief. "Mold will grow like crazy on damp items."

We found Troy, the packout supervisor, in the garage, then asked if we could postpone due to rain.

Troy shook his head. "Sorry, but we've got two trucks and full staff here. We have to do it today. Even if we reschedule it might rain again next time." He added, "I've got to check inside for a minute; I'll be right back."

I felt powerless as I watched a disaster slowly unfold in front of me. It was beyond reason that moldy items would be carried through a driving rainstorm, wrapped, and then stuffed in a truck. I knew what would happen, both intellectually (mold grows on damp items) and personally (mold spores popped open on my wet scalp).

I looked at Wayne. "We have to move forward, right? Troy is right; rescheduling doesn't ensure it won't rain again next time. The movers might not return until January given holiday breaks and their record of not showing up."

Wayne exhaled slowly. "January is five months after the explosion; our home and our possessions will be even worse by then. If we move our possessions out, at least they'll be cleaned and stored in a safe environment over the holidays."

I nodded. "We have to keep going; staying still means going backward. But packout in a driving rain is unbelievable." I wanted to run far, far away.

I was terribly torn and anxious, and looking back now, I realize how frightened I was. I felt powerless to stop the disaster unfolding in front of me. I'd held such high hopes until this point. I believed as long as we got expert help and made it to packout and remediation then we'd be on track to returning home. Our possessions would be cleaned, our house would be cleaned, then we'd move home and start over. I lost some of that faith in the driving rain, and I began wondering if we really had expert help. It didn't take a rocket scientist to guess it might rain during packout, so why didn't they have an event tent for coverage? I continued trying to believe in them, but the first morning of their first day of work was not a good start.

Troy found us stewing in the garage. He pulled down his mask. "Listen. We need a staging area. We need an area to wrap big items before they are loaded. We need permission to use your garage."

"But our garage is perfectly clean," Wayne insisted. "You can't bring moldy items in here. We don't want it contaminated."

"We'll be careful. We need a dry place to work. We can't wrap up your furniture in the rain and load it in the truck," Troy answered.

"No, that definitely won't work. Listen, we can't lose our garage; it is completely clean now. We need to keep it that way." Wayne was adamant. The garage was full of tools, equipment, a weight machine, files, and countless other items. We'd moved our desks into the garage as well.

I knew better than to chime in. Wayne told me many times how important it was to keep the garage clean so we could work and store cleaned items there. I knew his struggle was the same as mine. We had to do what was necessary to ensure a successful packout, but the idea of moldy items placed in the garage pushed him way past his comfort zone. But we had to avoid packing damp, moldy items at all costs.

Wayne took a slow, deep breath, then faced Troy. "Make sure they are careful."

I walked in the back door and immediately pulled my mask

down to cover my nose and mouth. While the air smelled horrible, I was pleased there still wasn't visible mold growth. No growth on the walls, ceiling, anywhere. The air still shimmered with mold spores that hung suspended in the thick air. I hoped this would be the last time I'd ever see Jell-O air.

Unlike the first testing crew, the packout team was dressed for work. The living room was a sea of white Tyvek. Photo albums and books were placed in banker's boxes, labeled, taped shut, then carried out. Lamps were wrapped and packed. Our beautiful oak antique armoire was wrapped, taped, placed on a dolly, and wheeled away. Same with the leather couches. They rolled up the forest-green area rug I scored at Pottery Barn. I was relieved as I watched them work—they looked diligent and professional. I hoped they'd be equally diligent while cleaning our items at the warehouse.

I decided to stop staring and get to work. I couldn't control the weather or the packout now that it had begun. But I could ensure that no confidential or proprietary work materials left my office. I got to work.

I tossed unnecessary confidential or proprietary papers into a four-foot-high brown burn bag, and left important non-sensitive files for the team to pack and store. When the burn bag was full, I covered the confidential materials with a layer of magazines, then pulled the bag to the kitchen, where workers were emptying cabinets. While dragging a second burn bag to the kitchen, I saw a worker leaf through a *National Geographic*, then put it on the counter with other magazines. I simmered back to my office, then searched for Troy.

I pulled down my facemask, "You told me everything in the burn bags would be burned. That guy is pulling things back out." I nodded toward the worker.

Troy spoke to the young man in Spanish and then turned to me.

"He says he likes these magazines and if you don't want them, he'd like to take them home. You *are* throwing them away."

"Yes, but I need to know that everything will be burned; not *reviewed* and *then* burned!" I exclaimed. "Listen, I don't care if he takes magazines, I just don't want anyone taking any other paper *besides* magazines."

Troy nodded and relayed instructions to the young man, who smiled and patted the magazine pile.

I found the situation surreal. They told us they would wipe down every page of every book to be safe from toxic mold, but it was okay for this guy to carry home a pile of magazines? *Are the magazines safe or not? Which is it?* I felt I had little choice but to stick with the program in progress, so I returned to my office to sort through sixteen years of work material.

I began feeling disoriented, so I walked to our bedroom to take a break from sorting. I opened my top dresser drawer and took out the two-inch wooden doll carriage I'd treasured since childhood. I twirled a blue wooden wheel and pushed the red fabric canopy back and forth, wondering if I should clean and keep the toy instead of trusting the remediators. The tiny china baby doll was dressed in a white gown and bonnet. This carriage and baby were more precious than jewelry; it had belonged to my grandmother. I tried to reason with myself, then verbalized this mantra: *The remediators are mold professionals; I have to follow their instructions and let them do their work. If every family member kept treasures, we might never be rid of the mold.* I placed the baby in the carriage, then put the carriage back in the drawer. I slowly shut the drawer.

I walked through the house to see how Wayne was doing. The

air-conditioning was turned off so it was hot and humid inside. I lifted my mask a few inches off my face to release my breath's moisture, then placed it back over my mouth. Workers were everywhere, wrapping up items and putting them in boxes. Bed frames, couches, armoires, rugs, lamps, dishes, tables, and chairs were wrapped up, walked through a few yards of pouring rain, and loaded into trucks. They wrapped up my recent Mother's Day gift, a Sharper Image massage chair. *I wish I could take several handfuls of valium, get in that chair, set it on high, and forget all this.*

I heard women's voices chattering in Spanish in Christine's room. When I heard "Precious Moments" I realized they were packing her Precious Moments collection. My mom sent a figurine to the girls for every birthday and Christmas. Shelby lost interest after a while, but Christine loved mementos. Christine was intent on saving the figurines for her own future daughters. I turned to continue looking for Wayne.

As soon as I walked in the garage, Wayne rushed over. "You're not going to *fucking* believe what just happened," he hissed.

I grabbed his arm and pulled him away from the workers. "Be careful; they can hear you!" I whispered.

"I don't care who can hear me!"

"Wayne, what happened?" I'd never seen him this angry.

"Well, that idiot over there," he nodded at a woman on the garage floor holding a vacuum cleaner hose. "She vacuums stuff off before it's packed. Well, apparently the vacuum got clogged."

He scowled. "I was way on the other side of the garage and saw her unhook the hose, look in it, then shake it. Then she turned the vacuum on backwards to get rid of the clog. Before I could get over to stop her, I saw a huge plume of toxic dust shoot straight up into the garage. So now our *garage* is contaminated!"

Wayne rushed over as Troy walked inside the garage. "You told me they were trained. You told me they knew what they were doing. Well, they don't!" Wayne swung his arm in a long arc from the back to the front of the garage. "They just contaminated my garage. Now you're going to have to clean my garage, and clean all the contents!"

"Yes, Mr. Milberger, we'll take care of it. We'll clean everything up," Troy replied quickly.

And it was *still* pouring like crazy. It was almost 8 p.m. before the last packed truck slowly turned out of our driveway. Wayne and I pulled off our Tyvek suits, locked the back door, then left for the bed and breakfast. I wanted a hot bath and deep sleep. While far from successful, at least the packout was over. Our important first step was over. The remediators would clean and store our possessions, then begin cleaning our house. Exhausted, Wayne and I drove to the B&B for dinner and much-needed rest.

I summarized our conversation with Troy about the garage contamination, then faxed it to CleanHome. Troy had agreed to send a crew to HEPA vacuum all exposed surfaces of our garage and spray them with biocide. They'd also agreed to clean our office furniture and equipment and move it to the portable building where Wayne and I would work. I faxed the summary because we were past the point where a conversation and my notes would suffice. Packing out in the rain and contaminating our garage put us on high alert; this process had not begun well. Every request, problem, or status summary would be in writing from now on.

We finally met Kevin, our new favorite insurance adjuster, for the first time. He was trim, nice-looking, and dressed in a blue button-down and Dockers. He took pictures in the house, then we returned to talk in the garage.

"The clothing purchased since you moved out will be paid for since you couldn't get clothing from the house," he began.

"Wow, that's great." I nodded.

"Your mattresses and pillows will be cashed out as well," Kevin continued.

Wayne asked, "What does 'cashed out' mean?"

"It means we believe they can't be cleaned so you'll be paid for them," Kevin responded.

"Oh, thank goodness," I exclaimed. "There's no way pillows and mattresses could be cleaned."

After our update, I walked Kevin to his car. He opened his door, then turned back to me. "You know, you guys are really nice people and are trying hard to do everything right." He glanced down, then back up at me. "I know you're upset about how the packout went, but I don't want you to end up like many other mold cases. Some people end up getting really paranoid and they never get over it even after remediation is complete." He paused, then said, "Mold isn't that big of a problem. We just need to clean your house and your possessions and you'll be fine. I hope you don't mind my saying this."

I knew he meant well, but was surprised by his words. "I appreciate this, Kevin. But I think contaminating the garage is a big deal. That was the only safe space we had left."

"You're right. That was a mistake, but they'll correct it. I don't want you guys to never recover, never get over it even after your house is clean. I've seen that with some people."

I struggled to process Kevin's comments as I watched him drive away. I didn't want to be overly paranoid, but was convinced toxic mold was a really big deal. Our mold made us really stupid quickly—too stupid to drive—how was that not a big deal? I was confident Kevin was trying to help and believed some clients remained unnecessarily paranoid after remediation, but didn't know how to not consider toxic mold a big deal. *Once our house and possessions were clean, I'll monitor my thoughts and actions in the paranoia department.*

A few days after the packout chaos, my middle child decided to go off the rails. Kim and Russ, our B&B hosts, asked me to sit with them. I watched their earnest faces and heard their words across the dining table, but had trouble processing them. I needed more time.

Shelby, my precious, fearless child, had asked Kim's adult daughter about birth control. Not how it worked. Not what it looked like. My thirteen-year-old wanted birth control without her parents' knowledge. I felt cold water swirl around me. I vividly remember repeating phrases over and over out loud, almost as if they were a warm blanket pulled against the cold. "Maybe she's asking for a science project," I muttered. "It must be for homework." But I knew if Shelby was set on a goal, she'd ultimately find a way. She was contemplating a path she wasn't ready for, and I was less equipped than ever to wrestle her away. I couldn't keep up with our life of mold remediation and work as it was. And therapy, our go-to solution in the past, wasn't an option given our remote location. Shelby's therapist was several towns away.

That evening, Shelby pretended to listen to me say she wasn't emotionally ready for sex, that it could bring up strong feelings and expectations outside her capacity. She said she understood and was gathering information for later. I hoped that was true, because I was less able than ever before to help her.

I felt like I was drowning. The feeling of not protecting my children was overwhelming.

My normal solutions were blocked by our remote location

and the excessive demands of remediation and displacement. My goal to safely steer this incredible spirit into adulthood just became more difficult. We hadn't returned to a clean home in months as expected. We didn't even have a completion date. Our displacement, plus the excessive demands of remediation, had weakened my ability to care for my children.

I prayed the remediation would be successful. We needed to return to our home, and normalcy, soon.

10

REMEDIATION BEGINS

The CleanHome crew began cleaning the house in earnest on December 18. They installed huge dehumidifiers that ran continuously. Two giant exhaust fans filled windows on either side of the house. The exhaust fans ran whenever staff was working inside. One exhaust fan was set up in Christine's window next to our side door, so the exhaust vented towards the garage and portable-building office.

I had asked about exhaust fans before we signed the contract; we'd already discussed placement and safety. I asked again when I saw the size and location of the fans. "Is it safe to have our mold spores sprayed through the neighborhood? This fan sprays directly toward our new office."

"Oh, yes," said buff Steve, the remediation supervisor we'd met when signing the contract. "The air is filtered before it leaves the house. Everyone uses exhaust fans during remediation; they are absolutely necessary."

"Wouldn't it be better if it didn't spray where we worked all day?"

"Well, we need to pull from both ends of the house. Don't worry, the air goes through a filter so it's perfectly fine," he answered.

The remediators cleaned our office furniture and placed it in our new portable building we'd use as an office. Wayne and I returned to work while the remediators began cleaning the house. This was a busy, hopeful time.

The kids, Wayne, and I were excited about getting away to see my family and possibly snow during our Christmas visit to Maryland. We borrowed suitcases from Wayne's parents and packed. I looked forward to everyone feeling normal for five days and forgetting about mold remediation.

I met with Steve before we left and he told me the remediation was going well. He said they'd finish before we got back from our trip. They'd remove the HVAC units and ductwork, since we had finally received approval to have that done. I was thrilled I didn't have to keep pushing, that the HVAC and ductwork hurdle was finally over.

Steve said, "No one can come in the house after we finish clean-up, not until the testers conduct testing. You can schedule testing for the first week in January."

When we returned from our trip, Wayne and I were excited to walk through the house after our first remediation.

"Wouldn't it be great if the house was totally clean?" I asked Wayne as we parked. "I mean, I doubt it would be completely clean, but wouldn't it be great?"

"It sure would." Wayne unlocked the door and we walked inside.

I was immediately struck by how eerily quiet the house was. Our feet echoed as we walked through the den and Christine's room. The kitchen was completely bare. The upper and lower cabinets, oven, stove, sink, dishwasher, and countertops were all gone.

I was happy we no longer had Jell-O air of packed mold spores. Unfortunately, while the air had improved, it was far from satisfactory. Instead of brain fog, I felt dizzy and light-headed in the house. The musty odor and its impact on our cognitive function were still noticeable, just less severe than before. The tile and grout were discolored in front of the refrigerator, but I didn't get on the floor to inspect closely. I learned months ago not to sniff around or breathe deeply. Short, shallow breaths, with minimum inhalation, were an automatic protective device at this point.

We walked through our offices and the living room, then headed down the hall. I gasped when we reached Justin's room.

"Oh my God! Wayne, there's mold growing on the ceiling!" I cried out. A two-foot circle of black fuzzy mold was growing on Justin's ceiling. I cringed and instinctively ducked my head, then shrunk away from the offending circle.

"What the hell is going on around here?" Wayne exclaimed. "Damn; there must be a roof leak. We replaced the roof just a few years ago."

"This is worse than before! We never saw mold growth until now, only smelled it. Now it's growing in the open."

"Well, there must be a roof leak. We have to get that fixed right away, so I'll make some calls," Wayne replied.

"We're going backward instead of forward." I backed out of Justin's room. The ceiling felt much lower now that it hosted fuzzy black mold.

I turned into the kids' bathroom and saw black mold growing on the wall next to their vanity.

"Damn. It's everywhere now." I scowled. I was crushed. The result of our first cleaning was visible mold growth, something that wasn't there before.

We inspected Shelby's room, then walked through our bedroom and bathroom. The smell was even stronger near our double sink vanity.

We exited the house and locked the door. We removed our Tyvek suits and masks, then washed our faces and hands.

I called Steve, the remediation supervisor at CleanHome, to tell him about the roof leak and other problems, then returned to a much-discussed topic, the attic.

"Steve, you know there are mold spores in the attic; they don't stop at the ceiling! It's humid up there, so mold will grow there. Now we have a roof leak and visible mold growth, so we *know* mold is growing in the attic as well. The house won't be clean until the attic is addressed."

"I agree. We can fog the attic," Steve responded.

"That would be great; thanks!" I paused, because there was more. "I'm concerned about the kids' bathroom. I'm glad the linen cabinet was removed, but there's mold growing next to their sink vanity cabinet. It must be growing behind the sink vanity as well."

"We can clean up visible mold growth, but can't tear anything else out until we get test results and the next remediation protocol. Sorry."

"I understand what you are saying, but that drags the process out." I was disappointed by this partial testing/partial cleaning approach, but I understood how the process worked. Remediators couldn't do more than what the testing protocol required. Testing firms and remediators had to be two separate entities; otherwise, they might do more work than necessary to spend insurance money. The remediators would clean mold off the wall next to the vanity, but wouldn't look for the mold source behind, or under, the vanity. That work had to wait for test results that found mold and a plan to fix the source of the mold—again. If tests weren't done under the vanity, nothing under the vanity would be cleaned. Again, the key to successful remediation was thorough testing.

I intensified my search for a better testing firm.

When I wasn't dealing with remediators, insurance, kids, or cleaning issues, I was working. My work kept me sane. Work was my respite; it was challenging, fun, and rewarding. I was working on a huge project with many meetings and reviews—I was grateful I didn't have time to dwell on the status of our house. I did what I could and was glad my responsibilities kept me too busy to worry.

It certainly helped that I was paid well. The flip side was that money wasn't solving the problem. Four months after the big rain, our first remediation was finished and there was no end in sight. We hadn't tested yet but already knew the house wouldn't pass testing. Nothing had been done on parts of the house that weren't included in the first remediation plan. Justin's ceiling was growing fuzzy black mold, and the kids' bathroom wall had visible mold. Not only was the process slow, we'd lost ground. Now the house had visible mold growth.

At least we had a clean place to sleep, eat, and work. I took a deep breath and plowed through the setbacks with renewed energy.

It was clear we wouldn't get to a successful outcome without a lot of effort on our part. The testers created a remediation plan that excluded the HVAC system, the remediators contaminated our garage while moving our possessions in a driving rain, and our first adjustor claimed complete ignorance of toxic mold remediation. If we didn't step up to fix these obvious lapses, as well as lapses we didn't notice, I was certain we'd lose our house to mold. We needed to continue gathering information on acceptable remediation standards and complain when our team failed to adhere to those standards or to common sense.

In a way, I'd been ready for this my whole life. Even as a girl I believed there was no guarantee things would work out and we needed fallback positions for those situations. My dad had a cool job and my mom didn't need one, how could they understand a quiet child's concern about growing up and paying bills on a fifty-cent-an-hour allowance? I couldn't even buy groceries for one meal based on my allowance; how much did adults make anyway? I remember when our family stopped in the desert for a restroom break during a cross-country camping trip. As I left the spacious, sturdy, clean concrete bunker restroom, I realized I could live in that restroom, it could be my safety-net. I was sure few girls exited public restrooms thinking about a safety-net. I left childhood determined to do my best to look after my future children. I was shocked that doing my very best for my children was not enough.

I would be more vigilant. I would find an excellent testing company to locate every mold source and target it for remediation. I'd monitor the remediators to ensure they followed the cleaning protocol. It was simple and it was doable; I'd certainly accomplished more difficult tasks. Wayne and I would beat this and life would return to normal. I had no doubt we'd be back home by summer. We'd definitely be home before school started in the fall.

11

BETTER TESTING FIRM

I called Kevin, our insurance adjuster, after our walk-through of the house. "We need a better testing firm. TESTX didn't do thorough testing, which resulted in limited protocol and cleaning. The testing firm didn't test or document the mold in the kids' bathroom. They said there was no evidence of damage in our bathroom vanity, which we know isn't true." I paused. "I've done lots of research and we want to use ViroTest testing. They are more thorough and professional. They cost more, but we'll save money because a thorough remediation will avoid a third remediation. What do you think?"

Kevin said he needed to check but thought it would be acceptable to switch testing firms. I alerted Liz, my ViroTest contact. She told me to send her the adjuster's permission letter and our current remediation plan. She added, "Let CleanHome know we will do the testing. If your adjuster balks, remind him your policy states you can select who conducts your testing."

"Thanks for the reminder." I was thrilled! Complete testing was the basis for successful remediation. Now we'd be on track to a clean home.

The following Monday I got the authorization fax from Kevin that ViroTest could conduct our testing. I faxed the authorization to Liz, then called to find out when they could come test.

"Austin can come test on Saturday," Liz responded.

"That's wonderful!" No one had worked on Saturday yet, so I was elated. Even though our lives had been turned upside down, everyone else continued with their normal workweek and nothing ever got done on weekends. I was ecstatic to make progress on a Saturday.

Austin arrived on Saturday, January 25. He walked through the house and immediately walked back out. "Listen, your house isn't going to pass, I can tell you that just by walking in. You still have a serious mold problem. Plus, it's raining outside, so that will make the results even worse."

"Test results are worse when it rains?" I asked.

"Yes, the humidity makes the air sample spore count higher, so it's harder to pass. To save money, I'll do a partial test today. We'll do enough to document what additional remediation steps need to be taken, but not waste money trying to get the house to pass. It won't pass."

I wasn't surprised Austin said the house wouldn't pass. It was awful inside. I was glad Austin offered his honest opinion and didn't want to waste our resources. This was an excellent start to our new chapter with a professional testing firm.

Everyone who visited our house commented about how bad it was—even people who didn't believe in mold's impact. Tony, a smart, burly friend of Wayne's, insisted that mold didn't bother him and said Wayne and I were probably just extra sensitive. Tony accepted Wayne's invitation to visit our house after our first remediation. After a brief tour Tony said he definitely understood what we meant by feeling spacy and disorientated in our house.

He said simply walking in our house "knocked him on his ass like three shots of whiskey."

Three weeks later, I was still trying to schedule the second remediation with CleanHome. I left a message for Steve, and the following Monday he called to say he'd fax the remediation request to me. A month after testing, and the next remediation still hadn't been scheduled. It was February. The process was taking far too long and we had so much left to do to get the house clean.

At least the roofing company came out to fix the roof leak. Now hopefully Justin's ceiling would stop growing mold. Unfortunately, Wayne couldn't be around during the repair. When he returned, he immediately noticed the ridge vent was puckering on the back corner, so he asked me to tell the roofers to fix it. I called and described the problem, and they assured me they'd return in a week to replace the shingles around the ridge vent. They also assured me they had caulked around the nail holes as Wayne requested.

Wayne and I hopped in his truck to go to lunch. We didn't have lunch fresh from the garden anymore. We didn't have time for a garden and didn't have a kitchen in the portable-building office either. I missed our fresh yellow squash, zucchini, tomato, onion, and basil dish. I didn't cook or exercise as much as I used to because I spent so much time driving to and from the B&B and dealing with remediation. We ate out a lot, but for some strange reason none of us gained weight. Apparently, stress was an effective weight-management tool.

We finally received the report containing our test results and the second remediation plan.

I immediately called Austin, the tester who wrote the report.

"The *kitchen* failed?" I asked. I felt like I was struggling to wake from a bad dream. All the appliances and cabinets had been removed and the kitchen had been professionally cleaned. The first remediation cost $10,000, but the remediated rooms still had mold! We'd never finish at this rate!

"Yes, the kitchen is high in Aspergillus and Penicillium, so they need to reclean the kitchen. They need to remove the attic insulation above the bathrooms and bedrooms at the far end of the house, and then HEPA vacuum all attic surfaces." He paused. "As you know, I didn't do a full clearance testing because I knew the house wouldn't pass. I collected air cell samples in several areas and tested all possible sources." Austin said he noticed that Christine's end of the house smelled really bad, but he couldn't find the source.

"Okay. Thank you, Austin." My eyes filled with tears as I hung up. I couldn't believe the kitchen tests still showed high counts of Aspergillus and Penicillium. The kitchen was the focus of this remediation, yet it still had toxic mold. *How will the house ever get clean at this rate?*

I felt my heart racing. I was shocked that the kitchen still had toxic mold, but more importantly, I was filled with frustration. Parts of the house still hadn't been targeted for remediation, yet CleanHome couldn't even clean targeted areas. I felt blocked at every turn. I had to fight to get critical parts of the house in the remediation plan, then had to fight to ensure that those cleaning efforts were successful. *Something has to change, or this house will never get clean.*

I drove into town and parked outside our insurance agent's office. I asked the receptionist if Bruce was available, then smiled weakly and shook my head when she asked if I had an appointment. Bruce was our neighbor as well as our agent. I didn't know him besides saying hi when we passed, but he was always friendly and personable.

After fifteen minutes, Bruce walked by and noticed me slumped in a chair. "Carol? What are you doing here?" His look of concern triggered my last remaining ounce of composure, and I started to cry. I was mortified; I'd never cried in public! Bruce took my arm and guided me to his office.

"What's wrong?" he implored.

"Bruce, I don't know what to do!" I plopped down in the chair across from his desk and told him the whole story. "Of course we failed the testing; we knew that was coming. But the real problem is the remediators aren't doing their job. The kitchen has a very high mold count, and it was their job to clean the kitchen!"

I wiped my eyes and focused on Bruce. "Between incomplete testing and incomplete remediation, we'll never get done. Their incompetence is costing *you* money and costing *us* time." I sat back for a minute, then continued. "Bottom line is we need a different remediation company. They can't even clean what they're *paid* to clean!"

I was surprised to see Bruce shaking his head. In a gentle, yet firm voice, he said, "No, don't switch from CleanHome now; that will let them off the hook for doing a poor job. Plus, then you'll have to start over with a new firm that may not be much better. CleanHome needs to do their job correctly."

"Well, you're right." I still wanted to fire CleanHome, but Bruce had a valid point. If everyone would simply do their job, then the process would work. Clean the house, pass testing, rebuild, then move back home. It seemed so simple, but it wasn't simple if people didn't do their jobs.

"Listen, I'll call the head office and let them know that the first remediation was incomplete due to incomplete testing, and that is costing more time and money. Also, I'll see if we can get you an extension on your additional living expenses, so those expenses will be covered longer."

"Wow, thank you. Do you think we need an extension?" I asked.

"Well, the limit on the value of your contents is set at the value of your house. Twenty percent of the value of your house is the amount allocated for your living expenses. Your living expenses coverage will last about eight months at your current spending rate."

He glanced down at his calendar and continued. "You have been out of your house five months, so yes, you may very well benefit from an extension."

I sat back in disbelief. "I had no idea it was going so fast. We've been so busy and Wayne handles those bills." We paid the B&B $110 per day for three bedrooms, two bathrooms, and use of the common areas. Not cheap for sure, but it was our best option. There was no more drama since the deer and raccoon incidents; we'd settled into a comfortable life there. But we'd expected to be back in our house in three or four months. Wayne and I needed to seriously reconsider our living situation.

I thanked Bruce for his help and we shook hands. As soon as I returned to our office, Wayne said, "I just got off the phone with Austin and our adjuster. We agreed that CleanHome needs to redo the cleaning at no charge. If it was on the protocol and didn't pass, they need to redo it until it's clean."

"Exactly," I agreed.

He glanced at his notes. "They need to remove and clean the ceiling fans; same with the light fixtures. They need to do a better job in the kitchen."

"Good. Maybe they'll get it right this time," I responded as I walked into my office to work before the kids got off the school bus. I hadn't scheduled time in my day for a public weeping session.

"That would be nice, wouldn't it?" he called after me.

"Yes, it would!" I called back.

I took time that weekend to call my mom while rocking on the B&B porch swing. I provided an update on the failed remediation, then stopped rocking to describe Shelby's low-key behavior over the last few months. "This could be a bright spot in the mold ordeal. Maybe Shelby stopped rebelling."

Mom chuckled. "That's possible. She noticed how busy you and Wayne are, saw the turmoil, and thought, 'Well, my parents can't handle much else.' Or maybe she thought she'd better stay close to home." Mom paused. "She probably wondered if she might get left next time you move! Goodness knows, you have enough on your plate!"

I smiled. "Right. I mean, what is there to rebel against? We aren't in our beautiful suburban home with a set schedule. Instead, it looks like a fight for survival against mold and various bad actors, including raccoons."

Mom exhaled softly. "I still can't believe you had raccoons coming up from under the floor! I've never heard of such a thing!"

"Me neither! I've never heard of most of the things happening to us!"

"You and Wayne are doing a wonderful job taking care of your family," she said warmly. "I hope Shelby sits back and watches the show instead of feeling the need to stir things up."

I resumed swinging as her tender compliment relaxed me completely. "Thanks, Mom. I certainly hope she does simply watch; things are stirred up enough!"

12

CAN'T USE TESTING FIRM

A week later Kevin, my adjuster, called with a progress update. At the end of the call, he said the insurance company was in litigation with Pam Steward, a microbiologist and ViroTest co-founder. He said the insurance company would probably require us to use TESTX for the next testing. They didn't want us using Pam's firm.

"That's terrible!" I paused. "Wait, Kevin. I thought I had the right to choose who performs our testing."

"Normally, yes. But I guess that's not the case when litigation is involved. This decision came directly from the home office."

"Damn. I can't believe it. They don't understand I *can't* use TESTX. I *must* have thorough testing. The whole thing is a joke without complete testing. Testing is the basis for remediation."

I was devastated by this news. I asked Kevin if he thought our house would ever get clean at this rate.

Kevin said, "Of course! You'll get through this and get back in your home. I've handled seventy mold claims and only have twenty cases pending. Mold claims usually take one to seven months to be resolved."

Kevin's reassurances made me feel better. I imagined how nice it would be to return home in seven months. Then I remembered we'd been out of our house for six months and the end was nowhere in sight.

I told Wayne the insurance company balked at letting us use ViroTest. He agreed it was our right to choose our testers; we'd been told that from the beginning. We wondered if results from a firm we hired would carry the same weight as results from a firm the insurance company hired. Despite these concerns, we decided I should fight for our right to hire the best testing firm. It was exhausting, to first learn the rules, then fight to ensure those rules were followed.

I was thrilled when the insurance company told us back in September that they'd cover our claim. I was ecstatic that the bills would be paid and we'd have support, quality information, and guidance. At that time, I thought we were a united team facing our toxic house. Now I felt like team members—the initial testing firm, the first adjuster, the remediators, and now our insurance company—had taken a giant step back away from our house, leaving us standing alone against the mold.

Later that day I called Steve at CleanHome. He didn't answer, so I left a message asking when we'd begin the next remediation. Wayne called him the next day, and I left a message again the following Monday. By Wednesday he hadn't answered, so I had the receptionist page him.

"Steve, we need to get going on the remediation. It's been three months since the last remediation finished," I began.

"I agree, but I'm waiting on approval from your adjuster. I can't get started without it," Steve replied. I left a message with Kevin asking about his approval of the remediation plan.

I called ViroTest but both Pam and Austin were out. We'd

vented toxic mold from two bathrooms into our attic, so I asked Liz to determine the best way to clean it. I asked if we should remove insulation above those two baths, or from that end of the house, or from the entire attic. Surely there was an approved plan for cleaning attics; this wasn't the first mold remediation they'd done.

The next few days were productive. Our AC Company removed the ductwork from the attic. A contractor came out to provide a bid to rebuild our house. Unfortunately, he said our house stunk, and we should gut the house and start over. While not pleasant news, it certainly confirmed what I felt.

I called Kevin again. I wanted to find out why February's remediation plan hadn't been approved almost a month later.

Kevin replied, "I have bad news. Headquarters says you cannot use ViroTest." He paused. "If you insist on using them, you will pay for the testing and we will have another testing firm there at the same time."

"What happens if the results from the two firms aren't the same?" I waited, then jumped ahead when he didn't answer. "Listen, Kevin, I was told early on that we have the responsibility of overseeing the remediation; but InsureUS keeps putting conditions on us. Can I talk to someone else about this? I don't want to be a pain, but testing matters. Testing drives the whole process!"

"Let me see if you can talk to the person overseeing your claim."

I immediately called our agent. "Bruce, can you find out why we can't use ViroTest?"

"Sure thing. I'll check and call you tomorrow." *Bruce, my hero!*

Later that day I called Liz at ViroTest for more detail. "Pam was deposed in a case involving your insurance company once. However, neither ViroTest nor Pam have ever been sued. I don't know why your insurance won't let you use us for testing."

Liz provided additional advice. "Ask them to put in writing why you can't use ViroTest. That should do the trick. If they put it in writing, you can take it to the State Attorney General. They aren't allowed to tell you who you can and can't use for testing."

As it turns out, I didn't have to take her advice. Kevin called the following day to say the home office reversed their position and would allow ViroTest to conduct testing. I was so relieved. I wished I didn't have to push for every little victory, but at least we could continue using a reputable testing firm. Maybe we would get through this ordeal after all.

While mold filled our home's air, an ocean of ladybugs descended on the girls' room at the B&B. We spent a magical, relaxing weekend watching tiny red spots crawl up, wander down, and disappear in the folds of the floor-length lace curtains. They crept along the hills and valleys of the comforter bunched across the unmade bed. They rambled along the headboard and climbed the four bedposts. A daring few struggled to take flight across the room. I didn't realize how much we missed having pets around until the girls tried naming the ladybugs. Even Justin plopped in the armchair to watch the show. Adam, the chubby stuffed dog, seemed to enjoy the excitement and extra attention in his own quiet way. The tiny bugs were mesmerizing—much homework was ignored during ladybug weekend. We were disappointed when they disappeared as suddenly as they arrived. Wayne and I missed them as much as the kids did, and checked several times over the next few days to see if they'd returned. I wished our mold would disappear that quickly, but clearly that wasn't going to be the case.

Wayne and I continued brainstorming ways to get closer to home. We thought the quality of our remediation would improve if we were on site. We were certain the remediators would take more care if we were around to ask questions and watch their comings and goings. We didn't have enough information about why the remediation wasn't working, and the best way to gather information was to be close by. Plus, we needed to cut costs and spend less time driving. Christine would be a senior next year. The extra hours on the road were cutting into precious time we could spend with her during her final year in high school.

"What about putting a travel trailer in the yard?" Wayne asked. "That way we can be right there for the build back and keep an eye on things."

"You mean a camping trailer on wheels, pulled by a pickup truck?"

Wayne nodded.

"We won't fit in a travel trailer."

"Well then, we'll get two travel trailers," he smiled. "If we're there all the time, I can plant a big garden. We can start eating fresh food again!"

"That would be awesome!" I paused. "Do you think our neighbors will mind the trailers?"

"Our neighbors are nice and everyone feels sorry for us. Plus, it would be temporary while we rebuild the house. I'll ask if you want."

"That would be great. It would be wonderful to be close by when we start rebuilding." I was starting to like this idea. I'd heard that travel trailers were prone to develop leaks over time, but Wayne assured me that he'd check and maintain them faithfully. He said travel trailers remained waterproof as long as fittings were tightened and seal quality checked.

The kids were thrilled with our plan.

"That is so cool!" Shelby and Christine responded almost in unison

"Excellent. We can spend less time driving," Justin added.

"We still aren't sure, but want to hear what you think first," I added.

"We think it's great! It will be like camping out!" Christine summarized.

I told Kevin we were thinking of moving out of the B&B so we could be close to home and oversee the remediation and rebuild. Kevin agreed that moving closer home was a sound plan. I told Troy we needed more things back, things like dishes, pots and pans, utensils, linens, and other items. Troy said they still couldn't find the sleeping bags we asked for. I located the sleeping bags box and room number on our 110-page list of our possessions, then reminded Troy they needed to be cleaned before bringing them back to us. Troy assured me he would get them cleaned and set up a delivery date. Our kids needed the sleeping bags for camp, so I needed them delivered soon.

ViroTest tested our house on April 4; our third testing. A week later Austin provided us with preliminary results. Approximately two-thirds of the house passed, but Christine's end and the kitchen failed. Christine's bedroom, the bathroom, and the den still smelled terrible, and the kitchen still had a high mold count. I called ViroTest to try to figure out why Christine's part of the house smelled worse than when we moved out. I wanted to know how mold was thriving in our house without a water source.

I finally talked with Austin a few days later. "Listen, Austin, Christine's room smells *awful*; much worse than when we moved out. Something bad is growing in there."

"Unfortunately, we found Chaetomium in Christine's room and her bathroom. Chaetomium is as toxic and dangerous as Stachybotrys." He paused, then added, "Also, we found

Stachybotrys on her shower floor, and growing under the bookcase outside her shower."

I was devastated. The nightmare continued. How could Stachybotrys be growing on her shower floor? Her room wasn't even close to the original source of the mold outbreak.

All we could do was take it day by day, not reflect on the past or future, but keep pushing for progress every day.

After many conversations, Wayne and I decided to move two travel trailers to our yard when the kids got out of school for the summer. Wayne filled me in on his latest find while washing dinner dishes in the spacious B&B kitchen.

"Bruce found a really nice travel trailer for us. It's thirty-six feet long, has three pullouts, and is practically new."

"You mean Bruce, our insurance agent? How did that happen?" I dried plates and wondered if there was an award for agent of the year. If there was, certainly Bruce would be a contender.

"I told him we were looking for a travel trailer and he said he'd ask around. His friend bought a trailer, used it two nights, then decided it's too nice to park at a deer lease." Wayne put the forks in the dish drainer. "We can go look at it. It has everything: microwave, stove, oven, refrigerator, and shower. It even has a fireplace!"

"Sure, let's look at it." We didn't need a fireplace, but it sounded nice.

It was getting close to the end of school, so I left a message for Troy to find out when we'd get our sleeping bags. A few days later I learned Troy didn't work there anymore and Ryan was the new warehouse manager. They certainly moved staff around a lot; it was like a revolving door over there.

On Wednesday we met with Steve and another muscular, polo-shirted remediation employee to discuss our status. Wayne and I wanted to know why the tile in front of our refrigerator hadn't been adequately cleaned in spite of numerous requests. The head of the testing firm thought the high kitchen mold count was due to mold growing in the grout and possibly under the tile, so she wanted all the kitchen tile removed. We wanted to know why Christine's end of the house was failing. It smelled terrible in her room and the den, much worse than when we moved out. This didn't seem possible if there wasn't a water source feeding the mold.

We agreed on a plan going forward, including a compromise regarding the tile in front of the refrigerator. CleanHome would pull up the baseboard and remove the wall behind the refrigerator, as well as the last two rows of tile under the refrigerator. If they didn't find visible mold growth, they would stop pulling tile. If there was mold growth, then they'd continue removing tile and thoroughly clean the area.

I saw one of the roofing company employees in town, so I asked when they would finish our ridge vent. He looked surprised and said he thought that had been fixed. Tears sprung to my eyes, but I blinked them away and explained we had mold. They had fixed our roof leak in January, but I'd been trying to get them to fix the ridge vent for months. He promised they'd come out and finish next week. Once again, I was reminded of how stressed I was. A five-minute chat with an acquaintance outside the post office almost resulted in public tears.

Before I knew it, it was time to move out of the B&B. Wayne and I planned to drop the kids off at camp, then return to move everything from the B&B to trailers. When we picked the kids up in mid-June, we'd return to trailers in our yard. I was thrilled to provide our children with three weeks of camp without mold drama. Looking back, Wayne and I could have used their help packing and moving, but I was adamant about providing as "normal" a life as possible for them.

Once school let out for the summer, the kids spent lots of time in their rooms packing for camp. I printed camp checklists for them to track what they had and what we needed to buy. Since we barely had the basics, we'd spend lots of time and money at Walmart that weekend. Bug spray, sunscreen, rain jacket, sweatshirt, "modest" swim suit, flashlights, eight pairs of everything (eight pairs—are you *kidding* me?), two water bottles, swim shoes, those infamous sleeping bags I fought so hard for, and much, much more. While they packed, I packed so we'd have less to do after dropping them off.

Wayne emptied the utility trailer so we could thoroughly clean it over the weekend. "It has to be spotless, immaculate, before we can store our clean clothes and everything else in there."

On Saturday, we packed and cleaned for hours, then spent more hours outfitting three kids at Walmart. We returned for our final night at the B&B. After a five-hour drive to drop kids off at camp in the Texas Hill Country, Wayne and I returned to move out of the B&B, then set up our new wheeled homes.

13

TRAVEL TRAILER LIFE

Wayne positioned the girls' travel trailer in the front side yard until workers could cut down a huge pecan tree and trim branches from another pecan in the backyard. Wayne always referred to pecan trees as "self-pruning," which I finally learned was Texas lingo for "Don't sit near them when it's windy." Branches as wide as me, or even the entire one-hundred-foot tree itself, could crash down without advance notice. We did not want to sleep within the radius of those trees. When the limbs were trimmed, Wayne would park the girls' trailer next to our big RV trailer in the backyard. Their trailer was currently situated too close to the road and too far from our trailer for my taste.

Wayne set up the big RV trailer in the backyard behind the garage, out of range of tree limbs. Wayne and I would sleep in the bedroom, and Justin would sleep on the pullout couch in the living room. Wayne hooked up the electricity and tied the trailer into our home's septic system. I loved the new trailer; it was gorgeous and spacious. I couldn't believe it had a fireplace! We didn't need one, but it certainly seemed like a fancy home on wheels. Wayne and I looked forward to overseeing the final clean-up and rebuilding of our house, as well as not spending one and a half hours commuting every day!

The girls thought they were totally cool having their own trailer, especially since it was parked far away from ours. They confessed they pretended it was their college apartment and chatted until the wee hours about how cool it was living in their own place. I hated that they were out of sight and close to the road, but it was temporary until our trees were trimmed.

The neighbor kids immediately arrived for travel trailer tours hosted by our kids. Entranced by our living situation, they rushed home to ask their parents if they could live in travel trailers in their yards as well. (Needless to say, no one followed our lead.) The fancy trailer was parked away from the road; after the tree trimming, both trailers would be almost hidden behind our garage. Of course this was temporary; it wasn't like we wanted to live in our yard. We wanted back in our house more than anyone!

Wayne and I loved being close to home, and regaining the hours we spent driving was wonderful. I started cooking even more since I had more time, and we had dinner together every night in our trailer. Life settled into a still busy, but slightly less frenetic sense of normalcy, with renewed hope that we'd return to our clean home. I even hoped for a fall garden.

I felt guilty we wouldn't go on summer vacation for the first time since our kids could remember. The tradition started with my parents, and I never intended to break it.

I wanted my kids to feel loved and valued that summer, but it would not be the result of a summer vacation. I was swamped with work and mold remediation oversight. I wanted them to return to morning swim team practice, but struggled to carve out time to drive them. Justin and Shelby rarely attended swim practice after Christine's activities kicked in. Shelby was so excited about swimming, she chose swim camp over church camp that summer. She was devastated when we learned her three-week absence violated attendance requirements for the relays. I questioned the ruling, but years of participation and team involvement couldn't sway the decision. Shelby lost interest in swimming after she was ineligible for relay events. I was disappointed—swimming provided great exercise and a clear start to the day—but I didn't have time or energy to do more. The old me would have checked the relay guidelines before booking a three-week camp. However, the new super-busy, super-stressed me did less checking and more acting and reacting.

I still travelled for work. In addition to Houston meetings, I presented training on administering the structured pre-employment interview for plant employees. With travel, this training sometimes became a four- to five-day trip. After a week-long June absence and a long drive home, I looked forward to decompressing and spending the weekend catching up with Wayne and the kids. The delicious aroma of freshly cut grass drifted through the car's AC unit, so I slowed down and opened the car windows to enjoy the warm air, then enjoyed a restful weekend catching up.

Longtime friends Roger and Debbie drove from Houston to spend the night with us in our trailer. We grilled steak and chicken on the Weber grill, then added squash casserole, fresh tomatoes, and steamed green beans. We ate on the iron patio furniture set in the shade of towering pecans, and drank, talked, and laughed until well into the night. It was wonderful to enjoy an evening with great friends in spite of our unusual living situation.

For weeks I pestered the testing firm to test the house, always receiving a variety of excuses and delays. I finally left a pathetic message on Austin's answering machine. I asked when he could come test our house, reminded him we needed to know their remediation plan for the kitchen floor tile, then finished with a pitiful plea, "Come down, we'll fix dinner for you. You can test the floor. Wayne will pull up the tiles so you can test under the tile as well. It will be fun! Call me, please!"

At least begging and travel trailer dinner invitations still worked. Austin called to provide a remediation plan for the refrigerator tile, which was to fumigate the area for thirty minutes, seal the tile, then check if the kitchen still smelled bad. When Wayne and I checked the kitchen a few days after fumigation, I immediately felt dizzy, like my brain was swirling in tight circles inside my head. The effect was so strong I placed my hand against the wall to keep from falling.

Wayne scanned the empty kitchen. "It smells terrible in here."

"I agree. There's not enough good air to breathe. I can't stay in here any longer." I turned, then walked out. Wayne followed, locking the door behind him.

"It's silly to lock the door. No one wants to be in here." I was only half joking.

"We have a duty to protect the public from hazards on our property. If this house isn't a hazard, I don't know what is!" Wayne was only half joking as well.

Wayne called Austin with our smell results and they agreed to move forward with the enhanced cleaning protocol. They'd remove floor tile in the refrigerator area, then clean the entire house again.

Two weeks later I called Steve and left a message asking when they'd begin cleaning. The following week I called him three times. Frustrated, I called our adjuster to vent about how we'd never get done, but he wasn't in either.

Wayne was still trying to get another large pecan tree removed and other trees trimmed. After several cancelled appointments he finally moved the trailers behind the garage so they were more hidden and closer to each other, but now both trailers were within radius of the edge of a huge tree. The tree company had assured Wayne they'd arrive in a few days—encouraging news. The other good news was the roof of our house was finally fixed. The bad news was that Hurricane Claudette arrived in the Gulf of Mexico July 13 and was heading for us.

At projected 90 mph winds, Claudette was a strong Category 1, almost a Category 2 hurricane. A non-event while living in our house, but high winds were an issue for travel trailers surrounded by monstrous trees. We'd tried to shield the kids from worry as much as possible, but that wasn't our focus as Claudette grew closer. Wayne told the girls to run the sink and shower water, and flush the toilet again and again. Shelby told me years later it was one of the most nonsensical dad-requests ever, but she gladly complied since his trailer hurricane preparation request was the perfect combination of both easy and silly. She happily flushed and ran water as she wondered what impact it could have. After he explained that a full waste tank provided ballast to weigh the trailers down, I earnestly flushed as well.

That evening we huddled in the large trailer kitchen listening to the driving rain and wind swirling outside. When a strong gust buffeted the trailer and caused it to sway way more than expected, the adults implemented Plan B.

I stood. "Kids, we're getting in the truck. Put on a jacket or a towel for cover, and let's run to the garage."

"What? Why?" Christine asked anxiously.

"It's safer in the truck," I responded. "Just until the wind dies down."

Wayne and I sat in front while kids and towels filled the back. Wayne turned on the radio, then immediately turned it back off. The deafening rain pounding on the metal garage roof drowned out all sound.

Justin leaned forward between Wayne and me, and half-yelled over the racket, "Dad, why is it safer in the truck?"

Wayne focused on Justin in the rearview mirror, "Justin, we're farther from the pecan trees here, so if one falls, it won't land on us. Even if the very top of a tree reaches us, we're protected by both the garage roof and the truck."

Justin sat back, and we settled in to wait amid thunder and pounding rain.

I remember being mesmerized by thunderstorms as a small child. I squished behind the living room couch to peer through the picture window to the cul-de-sac below. Heavy drapes blanketed my back as lightning filled the night sky and thunder bellowed through the house. I remembered nodding in silent support of the third little pig's admonishment to build a brick house. My parents' red brick house faithfully fulfilled its role, keeping us safe, warm, and dry.

But our moldy home didn't keep my family safe. I wondered how long the storm would rage. I wondered if we'd have to sleep in the truck that night. Why, with all our resources, why were we riding out a hurricane huddled in a truck in the garage? After all the hard work we'd put into our careers, we didn't expect to worry about trees crushing us in our sleep. It wasn't our fault the process took much longer than expected. Our remediation was progressing, even though it was slow. We really didn't have any choice on places to live other than the trailers and our contaminated home. I became even more determined to do whatever it took to get back to normal, soon.

Another week went by. I was sitting in the kitchen enjoying my first cup of coffee when Wayne climbed into our trailer with news. "The carpet was wet when I got up last night."

"What? What do you mean, wet carpet?" Wet carpet was like a wildfire or flash flood for all the damage it could cause us.

"The carpet outside the bathroom was soaking wet."

"What bathroom?" I really needed more time to process this news.

"Our bathroom; right over there." Wayne pointed to the carpeted step leading to our bedroom and bathroom.

"Shit!"

"I know. I checked in the storage area underneath the trailer, and it's wet in there as well. I found a leak in the seal around the shower drain. I replaced the seal and caulked around it, so it won't be a problem anymore."

"But the carpet is wet?" I was stunned; shaken.

"Well, I dried it with towels. I turned down the AC and I'm fixin' to get a fan to blow on the wet spot. That will dry it out pretty quick."

"What would we do if we got mold in here? Take it for cleaning? Sell it? Burn it?"

"Don't worry, it will probably be alright. I checked all other possible places for leaks: the roof, hoses, and fittings; everything is in good condition. I'll check the girls' trailer also. I checked when we moved here, but I need to check more often."

"Okay. Thanks!" I wanted to sound upbeat but was totally stunned.

I was grateful Wayne was on the job. If it was up to me, I'd have no idea what to check. All I could do was call people. Thank God for Wayne, he just kept fixing and cleaning. He discovered more problems, then repeated the process. It was exhausting. I just wanted to crawl back to bed.

Of course, there were times when I was less than thrilled with my husband. He started snoring a few years ago and was working up to becoming a world-class nighttime noise-maker. Usually, I could lightly remind him to roll over or change position and that would lessen the noise enough for me to fall back asleep. Sometimes that wasn't enough and he'd immediately return to snoring. He was very loud and almost shook the bedroom walls a few times while we lived in the house. I slept in Shelby's extra bunkbed on those nights.

I had fewer options now that we lived in a trailer. One night his snoring was deafening; surely he'd wake the neighbors. He must have been exhausted. Poking and prodding made no difference, he continued rattling the windows. It was impossible to sleep, so I grabbed my keys and a blanket, then climbed down to the dark yard. I was tired and frustrated and hadn't fully thought it through, but didn't have many options except staying up all night. Even my industrial-strength earplugs, keepsakes from numerous refinery site visits, were worthless against a Wayne snore. As I marched across the dark lawn in short PJs and Crocs, I suddenly felt nervous. *What if I meet a raccoon, or possum, or a neighbor's dog? More likely, what if I step in dog poop? Or slip in dog poop?* I hadn't expected dewy grass to brush against my ankles. By the time I made it to the office I was itchy and furious. I was furious with my options and furious with my choices. After inspecting my Crocs for dog poop, I pulled open the futon, yanked the blanket to my chin, and slept.

We were often sleep-deprived, but kept soldiering on. The next morning, I focused on moving our remediation forward. CleanHome had been incredibly nonresponsive. They never showed up for appointments. They didn't return calls. They weren't available when I called.

I stopping being polite when I called. If the receptionist

reported Steve was somewhere "around the building" I always asked that he be paged. My recent message consisted of "Steve! Get down here! We are sick of waiting!" I no longer bothered to maintain a professional demeanor. I felt like I was wading through waist-deep mud. My efforts didn't create progress, appearing instead to have no impact except to exhaust me. I was frustrated and tired of prodding remediators and testers. I wished they would simply do their jobs so we could focus on what was on our plate.

Steve simply stopped responding. He said they'd come work, but they didn't show. He didn't answer my calls. It took weeks for him to respond to my message. Supposedly he'd been in the hospital twice for kidney stones and his wife had a baby, but I finally believed they were making up stories to avoid us. Wayne finally reached Steve and scheduled an August 15 fogging, but they didn't show for that either. They only worked six days during an awful, nerve-wracking six-week period. Prodding and complaining had no impact. Nothing was done to fix our house. I watched, powerless, as our disaster dragged on in slow motion.

ONE YEAR LATER

A year after the big rain, we weren't remotely close to where I'd expected we'd be. Instead of being back in our clean house, or at least supervising the rebuild, our house still wasn't clean.

A year later, we slept in two travel trailers, officed in a portable building, and stored extra clothing in a utility trailer, all parked in our yard. Our fourth testing was held on August 29, and we expected the fourth remediation to start soon.

We didn't pass the fourth testing either. Our house was still infected with toxic mold.

The kids returned to school, with Christine beginning her senior year. A week into the semester, she asked me to get her childhood photos and school activity patches from remediation storage. Senior year traditions mattered to Christine, a senti-mental soul who took rituals seriously. Christine wanted her activity patches sewn on her letter jacket and childhood photos for a senior photo collage. Luckily Steve took my phone call, but questioned my need for the photos and asked why we couldn't wait—an unusual response. When I explained the photos were for a required senior year project, he agreed they were important and he'd ask someone to locate them.

I checked with the piano-cleaning company and discovered CleanHome had picked up our piano from them in May. I mentioned this to Wayne and we agreed it was strange, but imagined that our remediation had dragged on so long that CleanHome decided to cut storage costs. I didn't have time to pursue that question; my priorities were fixed on getting the house clean.

I'd pushed for wall cavity testing for some time. Standard protocol for most testing companies was to collect air samples from the room, and, in some cases, tape samples from visible mold growth or potential problem areas. With wall cavity testing, a hole is drilled in the wall near a problem area and a sample taken of the air inside the wall cavity. Since we still had toxic mold after four remediations, we needed to identify all possible mold growth. Kevin finally agreed it was the right thing to do, and we waited for insurance company approval.

A week later, Kevin called. "Sorry, but they're not going to pay for testing in the walls. We've tested all places that reported leaking. If you guys want wall cavity testing, it will be at your expense."

"I understand they are trying to control costs; I get it." I was disappointed but not surprised with this familiar pattern. I had to discover the necessary next step, then fight to get it done.

I called our insurance agent for his advice. After remediations in October, January, April, and August, our house still wasn't clean. Bruce offered to visit our house after lunch. We were hit with an overwhelming odor when we opened the side door and walked in.

"This smells terrible!" Bruce exclaimed.

"Yes, it's worse in Christine's part of the house than when we moved out. We need to test the wall cavity. We can't keep doing air samples and guessing what to do next. That will take forever at this rate!" I responded.

We walked through the house while Bruce took pictures. "Now I know what you mean. I feel 'funny' after only being here a few minutes! It's ridiculous how this is being handled. I'll call the home office to try to resolve."

"Thank you, Bruce; I really appreciate your help! Listen, I don't blame your company, they're just trying to control costs. But this piecemeal approach is killing us!"

Wayne later told me Bruce was shocked at how awful our house was. Bruce offered Wayne matches and said burning our house was the best solution, then immediately added that he was kidding. Wayne laughed and said he frequently talked about leaving a pound of bacon cooking on the stove, but we didn't have a stove. We also wondered if a fire was the best answer.

Bruce called a few days later to tell me the home office was taking a closer look at our situation. He said he dreamt he lived in our house, and felt terribly claustrophobic because he couldn't get enough air to breathe. I knew how he felt, I'd had that frightening feeling many times in our house. I remembered feeling scared, wondering if there was enough air to keep me, and my family, alive all night.

A few days later, our adjuster called.

"Listen, the insurance company wants TESTX to do additional testing at your house. Not wall cavity checks; just additional testing," Kevin said.

"They want to do a clearance testing? To see if the house passes this time?" I tried to clarify.

"Yes."

If the insurance company wanted to test the house that was their right; they paid the bills. After several attempts I contacted

Steve to find out when they'd finish cleaning so we could schedule testing.

"We have four more hours of cleaning to do, then we'll fog the house with the antimicrobial agent. You can schedule testing for Friday, October 17, or after." He paused, then added, "We'll want someone from our company at the testing as well."

15

TRAILER LEAK

On Saturday after dinner, I leaned down to put a pan in the cabinet under the sink. The bottom of the cabinet was soaking wet.

"Wayne, come look at this, please," I called with snake-finding, centipede-discovering fear in my voice. A snake pit would have been more welcome than a soaking wet cabinet.

Wayne came over to poke around, then calmly said, "Can you get everything out from under the sink and dry it out? I'll go see what's leaking."

Wayne found a valve under the kitchen sink that was a quarter-turn loose and creating a very slow drip. The kitchen was part of a "slide out" that extended out from the parked RV trailer. The bottom of the slide out was covered with a thick film to protect it from rain splashing up underneath. Unfortunately, that film kept moisture in the trailer as well. Since the valve was hidden under the film, Wayne didn't find it during his periodic trailer inspections. He only located it after ripping out the boards under the sink. He tightened the valve and put a pan underneath the offending pipe just in case.

Unfortunately, the trailer immediately smelled moldy. Wayne jumped into action early the next morning. He removed all the baseboards and the tack boards, but he couldn't get to the carpet. He tried to take it out, then tried to lift it up to dry, but couldn't access it.

"What will we do if it gets worse?" I asked.

"There's a large RV company in Houston that handles sales and service. I'll call them to see if they can clean it for us. Can you get everything out of here so they can clean it right away?"

I cooked Sunday dinner like always. The girls bounced up the trailer steps for a wonderful meal. I watched their faces fall as soon as they walked in.

Justin frowned as he stepped in the trailer, declaring, "EEEWW! It really stinks in here!"

When the girls looked up to gauge my reaction, I saw fear in their eyes. *Fear.* I was crushed. They knew that smell, and were afraid of what it meant.

"Hey kids, I know it smells bad, but we'll get it fixed. Don't worry. The RV place will clean it for us." I felt terrible, powerless to change our course, but was determined to remain positive for them.

"But where will you guys sleep while they fix it?" Christine asked, clearly worried. The stress was getting to Christine. Between her activities, homework, athletics, and other commitments, she didn't need even more mold drama. She had enough things to worry about.

"We'll move into the office until this is fixed," I responded.

"Where will you *sleep*?" she insisted.

"Justin will sleep on the futon in Dad's office; it opens to a bed. We'll move two mattresses in for dad and me. It will just be for a little while."

The kids ate in silence.

Wayne called the RV company and they assured him they could handle the cleaning. I packed up our clothes, shoes, dishes, food, medicine, and everything else. Wayne drained the trailer, tied everything up, then towed it to Houston.

We bought two twin mattresses for the portable-building office. Wayne slept on a mattress in his office, Justin slept on the futon, and I slept in my office. Each morning, I leaned my mattress against the wall and thanked God videoconferencing was in its infancy and wasn't the norm for business calls. Imagine how many shades of red I'd turn as viewers complimented my ivory-textured wall treatment, stopping in amazement when they realized there was a mattress behind me.

We cooked, ate, and showered in the girls' trailer.

Friday, October 17 was testing day! TESTX's tester expressed concern about the wall along the front of Christine's room.

"You've got a lot of mulch in the flower bed in front of the wall, and I don't see weep holes in the wall. If that is the case, there's no way for the wall to drain. I'm going to do cavity checks in that wall."

I spoke up immediately. "You're not allowed to do wall cavity checks; the insurance company won't pay for it."

"Yes, I can and I brought equipment to do it," he responded.

I was thrilled and relieved the insurance company's testing firm would perform the necessary tests. While happy about the progress, I wondered why, after four remediations, this wall had only now been identified as a potential problem.

TESTX did six wall cavity checks, seven air samples, and a few tape samples as well. Every wall cavity near a leak or possible leak was tested.

Wayne brought our big RV trailer home three days later.

They'd replaced the carpet under the cabinet and thoroughly cleaned the entire trailer. While most of the mildew smell was gone, we had headaches and felt dizzy as soon as we walked in. So, we cleaned it, then cleaned it again. Wayne vacuumed and wiped down every surface. Two days later Wayne and our house-keeper, Julia, cleaned the trailer again from top to bottom. (Julia felt sorry for us like many people did. She continued cleaning and helping us after we moved back to live in the yard.)

Saturday was a relatively dry day, so we opened the big trailer's windows to air it out. On Sunday Wayne checked and tightened fittings that may have loosened during transport. He replaced the air filters. We kept the AC on full blast to dry it out when the windows were closed due to rain or humidity.

The weather was starting to cool off, so I needed long-sleeved shirts and jackets from the utility trailer, the small white trailer we cleaned from top to bottom when we moved from the B&B. I was hit with a strong mold odor as soon as I opened the utility trailer door. I fell back on the grass in disbelief. It didn't make any sense; we'd thoroughly cleaned the trailer, then stored items directly from the dry cleaners. Nothing was stored that wasn't professionally cleaned. I quickly realized it didn't matter how it happened; I didn't have time to waste wondering about it. I had to focus on cleaning our winter clothes so we'd have something to wear, while ensuring nothing else, most importantly the girls' trailer, was contaminated in the process.

A few days later Wayne said he had a surprise for me, then led me to the medicine cabinet and mirror he'd installed in the garage bathroom. I almost started to cry; I was glad to have a daily mirror check even though I knew I looked awful. More importantly, I finally had a place for my toothbrush, toothpaste, and makeup. I hated leaving my toothbrush on the outside sink overnight in case a raccoon developed an interest in toothpaste. I didn't want my cup, toothbrush, and other toiletries on my office desk either, so I'd carted them from the portable building to the garage each morning. I was thrilled to be able to close them up in the medicine cabinet at night.

Thank goodness Wayne installed a toilet in the corner of the garage when we first evacuated. Otherwise, we would have been forced to traipse to the girls' trailer for every bathroom break. I wished he could have added real walls and a door, but we never expected to be using the garage toilet a year later. The tall, tool-filled shelves partially blocked the view, but it was far from ideal. He never had time to install a shower, so we all used the tiny shower in the girls' trailer.

Thank goodness my work was going great. I was so grateful to have an engaging outlet to distract me from remediation, cleaning, and tracking people down. After a phone update in late October, my boss inquired about Christine's senior year.

"I guess you're busy visiting colleges with her, right?" Janet asked.

I froze, and for a moment didn't fully comprehend her question. When my mind caught up with the outside world's calendar, I stammered a reply. "Oh, I can't believe it. No, we haven't even *talked* about campus visits! I wonder if she mentioned it but I didn't even hear her!" My mind raced ahead, wondering what else I'd missed. *Am I not hearing my children, or have they stopped telling me what is going on in their lives?* Both options made me nauseous; I never imagined I could let my children down to this degree. I certainly never imagined I could do so and not realize it was happening.

I willed those thoughts away so I could focus, then mentioned Christine was collecting college information and completing practice essays. I added, "She's reviewing applications, but hasn't mentioned campus visits."

"Oh, that's okay," Janet responded warmly. "There is still plenty of time."

16

PORTABLE BUILDING BEDROOM

Justin, Wayne, and I slept in the office for another month while we continued cleaning the big trailer. Wayne and I talked endlessly about additional cleaning protocols, whether the trailer could be adequately cleaned, and what we should do if it couldn't be cleaned. Wayne and I vacuumed and wiped it down countless times, and we aired it out for weeks during cool-weather days. On Tuesday I removed every item, stored them in trash bags, and wiped every surface with Clorox Clean-Up, again. We hoped the trailer would become clean enough for us to move back in.

Finally, we realized that might never happen.

Wayne did what he could, and bought another portable building so we'd have a place to sleep. Justin preferred sleeping on the futon in the office.

Wayne set up the new portable building on four cinder blocks in the backyard next to the girls' trailer. We figured this location was less obtrusive since someone driving by the house would see the gray portable-building office in front of the garage, possibly glimpse the two trailers parked behind the garage, but hopefully not see the new beige portable building next to the girls' trailer behind the house.

I never imagined we'd be in this situation one year and two months after the big rain. Not only were we not back in our house, but we were sleeping in a travel trailer and portable building in the yard of our contaminated home.

We'd invested over $70,000 in trailers and portable buildings. We'd invested countless hours cleaning, setting up, and recon-figuring our living conditions. None of these costs were covered by insurance, and of course our time was simply lost, and in many cases, wasted.

Travel trailer life took some adjusting, sometimes in surprising ways. I returned to the girls' trailer one afternoon to make dinner. As I stepped up to open the door, I heard the chorus to Alan Jackson's "Gone Country" blaring on the stereo. "She's gone country, look at them boots; She's gone country, back to her roots." Justin and Shelby were semi-watching TV from Shelby's bed, and Christine was fashioning Red Cross blood drive donation posters at the kitchen table.

I grew up on the East Coast in the sixties. The only country music I heard was when I walked by a garage repair shop. Back then I found the music and southern accents intolerable, and I remember tensing up for the inevitable long, loud wolf whistle, a sound that still makes me cringe. Suffice to say that country music was definitely not my preferred sound. I mentioned my dislike to Christine when she was fourteen, but she uncharac-teristically dug her heels in.

"Would you rather I listen to rap? That's what some of my friends like."

"No, that's alright," I mumbled. Score one for the respectful eldest child. I lifted my country music ban and eventually learned to enjoy some songs.

But the combination of country music while living in a travel trailer in our yard was too much for me. Trailer life was an adventure at first, but a year later, we'd lost too much ground to mold. My husband, son, and I slept in a portable building set on cinder blocks. The entire family was surrounded by laminate and plastic. I looked terrible, monotonously wearing old clothes, plastic shoes, and a haggard look. My insane stress level was likely causing me to miss large swaths of conversations; many facial expressions and cues were probably wasted on me.

This was no longer an adventure. I was not dreaming of going country. The song's lyrics grated on me; my roots were the D.C. suburbs, not the country, not a wheeled travel trailer, and certainly not a portable building. Yet here I was, making dinner in a travel trailer while listening to country music. If I had a bathrobe, which of course I didn't because it was packed in a cardboard box in a Houston warehouse along with the rest of our possessions, it would have completed the image.

I filled the stock pot with water, and chose my words carefully so they wouldn't realize I was flirting with a mental breakdown. "Guys, we need to change the music. I can't handle country music right now. It's too close to home, so please find something else." Shelby fiddled with the dial until she located a family favorite. I smiled in relief as "Brick House" blared through their trailer while Shelby and Christine wriggled and lip-synced.

We asked CleanHome to return Shelby's tall white ash dresser and matching twin bunk beds, our queen metal bed frame, a wine cabinet, and a few other things. We planned to use this furniture to set up our bedroom in the new portable building. We also asked them, again, to return our photos.

"Why do you need all your photos? Wouldn't you rather

wait until you are back in your house?" Steve asked during a phone update.

"Christine is a senior this year and each student has to make a collage of childhood photos. I have no idea which photos are where, so I'd rather get all of them back."

"We'll see what we can do," Steve responded.

I asked Steve to return our TV and VCR. I wanted to do yoga but there wasn't enough room in the girls' trailer. I tried stretching in the kitchen while facing the front door with my legs straddling the kitchen counter. When leaning over to reach my right toes I had to concentrate to avoid banging my head against the kitchen cabinet. Each time the kids walked in they had to stand between my legs, then gingerly step over my right leg, apologizing and letting me know they had to go back out again. I cringed as Justin's large sneaker swung over my head, then waited as he stood over me trying to unlatch the door to leave. I finally gave up after fifteen minutes. Travel trailer yoga, at least travel trailer yoga with three teenagers, was not relaxing at all.

CleanHome finished cleaning our house on November 7, then returned the following day to fog it. Wayne and I walked through the house with Steve a few days later. We were disappointed, to say the least. Christine's end of the house was terrible. As soon as I walked in the back door, my ears closed up, then I got a sore throat. Even worse, I was disoriented and light-headed after a few minutes of walking through the house. We told Steve about the smells and our physical reactions. He didn't disagree, but said he hoped they'd caught everything. He said we needed to wait for test results to locate the remaining mold sources.

We were caught in a repetitive cleaning and testing cycle. Our test company determined the possible mold sources, then the cleaning company cleaned those areas. The companies worked together and with us when trying to figure out the sources, but when the house failed, the remediator's first response was that the mold source wasn't identified by the testing firm. Until we received test results, we didn't know whether the mold odor and our physical reactions were due to inadequate testing or inadequate cleaning. We simply knew our house wasn't clean.

A few days later we cleaned the big trailer from top to bottom, again. On November 14, several tornados touched down in the area. We had warnings all day but luckily none of them landed near us. We felt like a tornado magnet now that we effectively lived in a trailer park. The next day we had torrential rains all day long. It was miserable having to run through the rain to use the garage restroom. The wind and rain were so strong it blew in under the closed garage door, soaking the floor two feet in, which was frightening as well. Our living arrangements were getting depressing.

CleanHome delivered some of our requested items a few days later. We were shocked at how dusty the dresser and bedframes were. Additionally, several requested items weren't returned, like our checkers table or photo albums.

"This wine cabinet is totally covered in dust! Everything is filthy! Listen, take pictures so we can show Steve," Wayne complained as we unpacked and wiped down each item.

"I can't believe they didn't wipe them off before returning them; they should be embarrassed to return them like this. We paid so much for cleaning and storage. I guess it got dusty sitting there for a year, but this is ridiculous," I responded.

"We've got to clean every surface. Wipe everything down, inside the drawers, all sides and the bottoms too before we put it in the new building."

"I will, I wish we'd bought stock in Clorox wipes," I added

as I wiped down every inch of a dresser drawer.

"We should have bought stock in bleach, and of course, Clorox spray," Wayne agreed.

Wayne and I moved the white ash dresser and twin bed frames to the portable building. We had moved some clothes and a few plastic totes in the prior week, and were looking forward to no longer sleeping on the office floor. Wayne had leveled the new portable building, hooked up electricity, installed a toilet and sink, and tied those into our sewer system. He hadn't hooked up the water yet.

On Friday evening, soon after moving the furniture in, Wayne broached the dreaded question that needed to be asked, "Does it smell funny in here?"

I didn't want to agree, but unfortunately, he was right.

I was devastated. I couldn't believe it, but agreed it smelled bad. I was already feeling spacy. I looked around the brand-new, virtually empty room. "It can't be the dresser or twin beds; they were professionally cleaned and we just got them back. We just wiped them down. The dresser is solid Ashwood, it doesn't have any particle board at all. None of these items have been wet—there is nothing for mold to live on."

Wayne offered a solution. "You know you can use a flame to attract dust in the air, right? I wonder if it would work with mold spores? Do you have any candles?"

"I've got a bunch of candles. I'll get them." I bolted out the door. I wanted to keep running, but adults don't do that to each other. Adults stay and help; they don't run far, far away when they can't take any more. However, continuing to run was my first thought as I blasted out the door.

We arranged votives under the ash twin bed, then lit every candle. We scooted candles so each flame sat under the frame or a wood slat. Darkness fell quickly while we crawled around the floor repositioning candles.

I relaxed against the wall, then noticed Wayne's chin flickering in the candlelight as he leaned under the bed to nudge a candle over a few inches. I realized we had sunk to a new low in our efforts to eradicate mold. We'd tried ozone, numerous cleaning supplies, black lights, increased air flow, high heat, air-conditioning, several professional remediations, and now, after all that, now we were relying on votive-candle smoke.

Either Wayne recognized my expression or reached the same conclusion at the same time, both products of an eighteen-year marriage.

He grinned, then leaned against the wall. "Maybe we should say a prayer to the mold gods?"

"Yes, we should definitely acknowledge they are in charge. I guess they expect an offering as well, right?" I snickered at my solution. "But what can we offer? The mold gods already have our house."

Wayne agreed. "And our big trailer. And the utility trailer. Looks like they want this building as well."

We sat for another ten or so minutes, in case smoke actually helped eradicate mold. Another ten minutes wouldn't hurt anything. Then we blew out the candles and shoved them against the wall so we wouldn't trip on them in the dark.

Sunday morning I walked into the office to wake Justin for church, and…the office stunk of mildew. I found Wayne.

"Hey, the office smells kind of bad." I tried to act calm, but my downcast eyes couldn't focus as they darted around the garage floor searching for an escape tunnel.

I shadowed Wayne as he walked through the office. He shook his head, then slowly turned to face me. "This is totally crazy. I'll change the air filters, but can't clean right now. I've got to pick up some things in town. I'll be back in a little while to help."

Justin and I skipped church to vacuum and wipe down every surface of the office.

Wayne returned hours later. "Wow," he said while stepping inside. "It's still bad in here."

I quickly responded, "I know. We've been cleaning since you left. I can't find the mop anywhere, so I still haven't mopped. It's not in any of the places Julia leaves it to dry."

Wayne deliberately scanned the room, then slowly walked to the far wall and opened the door to a ten-inch-deep broom closet (so small I forgot it existed). He pulled out our mop. Our *damp* mop. Our mildewy-wet-sock-smelling *damp* mop.

Wayne returned the mop to its normal drying location on the back porch. He and I replayed and replayed the obvious question. Who would store a damp mop inside? We always put the mop outside to dry in the sun. Even before our house exploded with mold, everyone, even the children, knew damp things had to be hung up or put in the sun to dry.

We questioned the kids one by one. Justin shook his head. No, he didn't use the mop and knew better than to store a wet mop inside. We repeated this scenario with Christine, then Shelby.

"Let me get this straight." Acting like she was leading the jury to an obvious conclusion, Shelby straightened, then faced us. "You're asking if I: 1) *used the mop,* and 2) *put the mop away*?" She paused to survey her imaginary courtroom, then demanded, "Do you realize who you are talking to?"

Her eyebrows arched. "When have you *ever* known me to touch a mop? And if for some reason I did use it, would I put it away without being asked to?"

I smiled in spite of our grim situation. Mold or not, this kid was destined to go far.

When Julia returned to clean the following week, we asked about the mop. She was as surprised as we were.

"I put it in the sun to dry on the back porch, like always."

"Julia, I know you did. I guess we'll never know how the wet mop got in our closet," I responded.

While I didn't know how the damp mop ended up in the closet, I had a pretty good idea of the impact it would have on our lives. Our office sat outside our moldy home. Add a damp mop in a closed closet and you've got the recipe for a disaster. Or the recipe for an additional disaster, since we were still dealing with the initial mold disaster, the loss of the big trailer to mold, and of course the failed remediations.

We finally received our photo albums and Christine's activity patches a few days before Thanksgiving. I sat outside on a clear day and pulled photos from behind the plastic overlay, then dropped them into a large plastic bin. I threw the empty albums away, packed the top of the bin with paper towels, then secured the lid. I smiled. We had our family photos back.

Thanksgiving dinner was held at Wayne's brother's house, a study of rustic elegance: sparkling glassware, layers of ornate china, harvest floral arrangements, and platters of beautiful food scattered across an impossibly gorgeous home. With the addition of family and a festive atmosphere, it was almost overwhelming. This visit was of particular interest to Wayne and me because his brother's house had just been remediated after a mold problem.

Wayne pulled me aside, "You don't smell mold or feel funny here, right?"

I whispered, "No, it smells and looks great. How did they get their remediation done in months?"

"They didn't have toxic mold, just regular mold."

I sipped rum and Diet Coke. "I wish we could have returned

home in months. Anyway, it's great to know people who recovered from mold—remediation *can* work!"

It was difficult to consider leaving their beautiful, spacious, clean home much later that evening. I remained burrowed deep in soft leather couch cushions until we'd long overstayed our welcome; unusual behavior for me. It was almost impossible to exit their festive, airy home, full of turkey aroma, mixed drinks, and comforting big-screen football commentary. If I had been a toddler, I'm certain I would have pitched a fit, clutching plush armchair legs and textured area rugs while being dragged to the car. But I was still mostly an adult and our kids were watching, so I let Wayne tenderly escort me to the car while the kids trailed behind. We returned to the travel trailer, the portable-building bedroom, the smelly portable-building office, the big RV trailer we refused to enter, and our contaminated home. Apparently, I missed the comforts of our old life.

We bought a freezer and a comfortable queen mattress. We struggled over the absurd mattress prices, but assured ourselves we'd move it to the house when we rebuilt in a few months. The following day Wayne spent $800 at Home Depot for our portable building bathroom. He bought a sink, mirrored medicine cabinet, towels, hot water heater, and other necessities. I was excited at the prospect of a nice comfortable mattress, indoor plumbing, a mirror, and hot water!

Cold weather arrived quickly; it was 35 degrees outside. That night I used the restroom in the garage, then returned to bed. I shivered under extra blankets even though I wore two shirts and two pairs of socks under my pajamas. The heat was on, but it couldn't keep up with the outside temperature.

I got out of bed to turn up the heat, then asked Wayne when we could use the inside toilet.

"It's ready now," he replied sleepily.

"Oh, thank God! Why didn't you tell me?" I asked.

"Sorry. I thought you knew," he replied and returned to sleep. He must have been exhausted; it was unlike him not to tell me what he'd accomplished each day.

I was concerned when I woke up with a stuffy nose. I didn't suffer from seasonal allergies, so this wasn't a good omen for our bedroom.

Once Wayne hooked the water up to the portable-building bathroom sink, I could brush and wash in our bathroom before bed. The water was really cold, but it was nice not to have to trudge through the yard to the garage each night carrying my toothbrush like a camper. *I didn't sign up for camping, especially winter camping.*

I made spaghetti for dinner Sunday night. As the large pot of water approached boiling, I noticed the trailer windows were fogged over. I'd made spaghetti tons of times in the house and the windows never fogged and I'd cooked spaghetti in the trailer without incident. Then I realized the cold outside air caused the humidity to build up in our small trailer. I wiped off a window with a paper towel, then noticed water pooling in the metal window well. *Did they have to call them wells?* I checked the next window and found another pool of water, then noticed water rivulets streaming down the front door. I took a deep breath and calmly asked the kids to wipe off each window. I followed behind them, pretending to be calm as I used paper towels to soak up water pools. I tried not to think about the possibility of water leaking from the windowsill inside the wall below. We had already lost one trailer; we simply could not lose this one. I soaked up water from the sills, then wiped the windows and door again. I could not manage another loss.

17

NO WAY THIS HOUSE PASSED

In early December I received a call from Gordon, the reptilian son of the remediation company's owner. I had only met Gordon once, but he made a huge impression when he arrived to collect a check months earlier. Wayne and I were scared, desperate for relief, drowning in mold, and hoping the owner's son would act to improve our situation. I watched Wayne plead with Gordon for thorough cleaning, while Gordon's cold-blue eyes focused, stone-faced, on the back wall of our cavernous garage. Gordon's neck veins rippled underneath his clenched jaw while Wayne talked. I tugged Wayne aside and whispered, "Stop talking, he doesn't care; he's waiting for you to stop so he can collect the check. He'll do anything to get that check." As expected, Gordon left as soon as he collected our money. We hadn't seen or talked to him since.

Gordon said Steve was in the hospital with kidney problems and wouldn't be back for a few weeks.

"I'm sorry to hear that." While I was sorry, I doubted young, buff Steve was in the hospital for anything. Either Steve had quit, decided to spend an entire week at the gym, or, most likely,

Gordon was lying to me.

"Your house passed the last test," Gordon announced firmly.

I inhaled sharply. "That can't be true. The house isn't clean. I get dizzy in…"

Gordon cut me off. "Well, it did pass. You'll get the clearance letter soon. We need our cleaning check for $11,004."

"But the house isn't clean," I protested.

"Yes, it is. It passed the testing, and you need to pay us," he responded firmly.

This demand sent me into a tailspin. Christine's room smelled worse than when we were ordered to move out fifteen months earlier. I experienced carnival-ride-level dizziness when I stepped in the back door. The house wasn't clean; anyone could tell you that.

I'd been playing catchup with insurance, remediation, and testing protocols since the beginning. Now the remediators said our house was clean but we knew it wasn't. Would this game of musical chairs simply end after fifteen months? The insurance money was disappearing. Would the remediators pack their equipment up and leave us in trailers in our yard outside a contaminated house? It wouldn't faze Gordon to do exactly that. All he wanted was the check.

I hit an emotional wall.

I cried almost every day that week.

Tears ambushed me without warning in private and in public. Deep pain launched out of my body in fits and spurts while I fought to regain control. I never knew when, or where, I'd erupt.

Sunday's sermon was on bereavement. Tears sprung to my eyes when our minister described bereavement as a state of chaos, where the bereaved deal with loss, disruption of routine, challenge of beliefs, life in turmoil, and loss of hope. I intensely blinked to suppress the well of tears rushing to greet her words. My tears, my cells, cried out. *This is us! She's talking about us. We lost our home. Our routine was disrupted. I questioned beliefs about science, sanity, and reality. I've lost hope.*

My shoulders released. I exhaled and relaxed against the wooden pew. I felt less alone as I heard my situation accurately described. I didn't realize I was in the stages of grief until that moment. Knowing countless others had survived similar pain, refueled my hope. I hoped additional knowledge would help us climb out of our mess. I blinked the remaining tears off stage before my children noticed. I had never cried in front of them and I wasn't going to start now.

The next day I called a podiatrist to make an appointment for Justin, who was complaining that his foot hurt really bad. He never complained of pain unless something was broken, and sometimes didn't complain then, so I knew he should be checked quickly. I burst into tears when the receptionist said we couldn't have an appointment without a referral from his primary care physician. Once again, my child needed something and once again I had to put them off. Once again, I was failing my children. My emotions were raw.

On Wednesday, I met my boss, Janet, at her Houston office. After working all morning, we chatted on her office couch before lunch.

"I watched the *Extreme Makeover* show last night and thought of Justin. You know the show where a family's dilapidated house is quickly rebuilt?" Janet glanced at me, "You've seen it, right?"

I nodded. "I heard it's a great show." I hadn't watched TV in well over a year, but there was no need to share that detail.

"The family is surprised with a brand-new, beautiful home. They have a boy who looked a bit younger than Justin." Janet paused to smile. "He cries and cries when he walks into his new room, complete with bunkbeds and a basketball net in the corner. It made me think of how happy Justin will be when he gets his new room."

My emotions erupted at her description. We were so far from a new room, and now even our clean air was threatened again. I had no idea how to get back to any of it. Without any warning, my pain exploded in tears.

I jumped up and walked toward the door while wrestling to regain control. I was unable to speak, and wasn't sure what sounds would occur if I tried. I reached the door, then circled back since I couldn't cry in the hall either. I returned to the couch and leaned forward to cup my head in my hands. When I was finally able, I apologized, "I'm so sorry! It's been so hard these last few weeks. I don't know what we're going to do!"

Janet was mortified. "No, I'm sorry; I shouldn't have brought it up! I thought things were going well."

"Things aren't going well. I can't talk about it." I took a deep breath. "I'm beginning to wonder if we'll ever live in our house again."

I couldn't describe our situation to her. I was the problem-solver at work, not the problem-creator. Janet's kind words had totally blindsided me. I could handle work problems all day long. I could even handle our problems for months and months, but words of encouragement stung terribly against our bleak situation. After a few minutes, I recovered enough to walk in the hall and enjoy lunch with her. I was glad to escape back into my work that afternoon.

Kevin, our adjuster, called a few days later.

"I got your clearance letter in the mail. Your house passed; it's time to rebuild."

His words caused the ground beneath me to shift—now our adjuster said we were done. I immediately countered, "The house shouldn't have passed. It smells, and I get dizzy as soon as I walk inside. It should have been gutted from the beginning. We can't rebuild until the house is clean."

"Well, the fact is, the house passed so the next step is to rebuild," Kevin responded.

"Listen, we can't supervise rebuilding a moldy house. If we walk out of that house without showering and washing our clothes, we could contaminate our trailer. We cannot afford to contaminate the only clean place we have to live. It is that simple."

I paused, then made an offer, "Does the insurance company want to buy it? We can't use it. If you guys think it's clean, then you can buy it and rebuild."

"Well, I don't think so. I'll get back to you on that."

I didn't expect the insurance company to buy our house, but it was worth a try. We certainly wouldn't live in it in its current condition.

Buff Steve called after his hospital or gym stay to explain our options. "We need proof that the house didn't pass. You need to get ViroTest out to test, and the house needs to fail. Otherwise, we are done."

"That makes sense." I was relieved for a path forward. Our testing firm would collect results showing the house didn't pass, but I still had no idea what would happen if the test results from two different firms didn't coincide.

I told Steve I was disappointed with the state of our returned items. "You guys need to do a better job cleaning our items. Most of the items you returned were filthy and covered in dust."

"They shouldn't come back dirty. I'll make sure your contents are clean."

Wayne and I were searching for houses to buy or rent in our school district but hadn't had much luck since there wasn't much available. I told each of the kids we'd begun looking for another house because this one might never get clean. Christine and Justin agreed it was the best option, although neither wanted to move. I was surprised when Shelby burst into tears at the news. Resilient throughout the ordeal, now she became unglued.

"I don't want to move!" she blurted through flowing tears. "I want to live in *this* house! And I want to take a bath!" Her head dropped to her hands as she sobbed.

I was devastated to see her this way, and struggled to find words to console her. "I know, honey. I want to live here and really want a bath also! But, honey, we've tried so hard, but it hasn't worked out. I'm sorry!"

"I want to live in our neighborhood! Why can't we tear down the rest of our house, and then rebuild? I heard you and Dad talk about it. That's what I want to do!" she begged with renewed energy at a possible solution.

"I'm sorry, but we can't keep living like this. It will take too long and too much money to tear everything down and rebuild an entire house. And this piecemeal approach clearly hasn't worked." I thought about how hard we had fought, all the effort, cleaning, money, and time, only to be worse off than in the beginning. I was becoming convinced that we needed to explore moving, no matter how hard it was on everyone. We had tried to remediate but failed on every attempt. We had to stop trying.

I faced Shelby. "I'm sorry, but we just can't keep doing this." I reached out to hug her, but she pulled back, folded her arms across her chest, then rocked back and forth, talking loudly. "What if we can't find a house in this school district? I don't want to change schools! Do you know how hard it is to change schools at my age?"

She exploded with another concern, clearly searching for supporting arguments. "Cats can't move because they are territorial! Our cats are attached to this house! If we move, they'll run away looking for their home and they'll never find us!"

"I know they are. I'm sorry, honey. But we can't keep living in these conditions. Dad and I have to look at other options. We'll try hard to stay in the same school district, but we will move away if we have to."

I was worried about her. I didn't expect her to be so distraught about moving. I hoped she'd soften to the idea, because we couldn't stay here. Goodness knows we had tried and failed.

No longer limited to meeting dates and notes, my spiral notebook had expanded to include what I called "our crazy ride." I wanted to document all that happened because I couldn't believe it while I was living it. The notebook also became a place to voice my fears and frustration. While not technically a "journal"—I didn't have time or energy for that—it helped to have a safe place to vent and voice my fears.

In mid-December Steve arrived to collect payment for remediating the house. I'd cleared the payment with our adjuster. Kevin said our house passed testing so we were obligated to pay for their remediation services.

I showed Steve my list of requested possessions, and highlighted the items that were filthy or not returned. Steve promised to return the missing items next week, and said he'd send people to clean and HEPA vacuum items as they were unloaded.

As I dated the check at my office desk, Steve added: "Oh, can you make it out to Spotless, Inc. instead of CleanHome? Customers started getting us confused with another company, so we had to change our name."

I stopped writing to think. It was their money, and the insurance company approved the payment. I figured it didn't matter how they wanted the check styled; their check, their choice, right? I glanced up and saw him standing in my doorway with his muscular arms folded across his broad chest. He wasn't menacing, just huge. I'd have a hard time getting past him. I decided not to try. He disappeared after receiving the signed check.

Wayne exploded when I told him about the name change. "What do you mean you made it out to a different name? We don't have a contract with Spotless, Inc.! I knew it!" He jumped up, then paced around the office. "They must have declared bankruptcy, now they're hiding money from their creditors! That is CleanHome's money, not some new company!"

"I'm sorry. He was really insistent!" I pleaded.

"I bet he was. I can't believe he asked you to do that." He ranted and raved for a while longer, then settled down.

I had high hopes for our mid-December visit to an adorable rent house. The house was small, but in a beautiful setting on the banks of a river surrounded by mature live oaks. Even better, it was on the school bus route and we knew several nice families in the neighborhood. I could feel my heart beat faster as Wayne drove up the long driveway and parked next to a row of thick azalea bushes. It was cute and in our school district; I knew this house would work for us.

While small, the first floor was clean and the kitchen dining nook overlooked a beautiful backyard. The upstairs bedrooms were adequate, and I was particularly thrilled to see closets again. I no longer required a walk-in; a glimpse inside a standard reach-in closet took my breath away. My hope evaporated when I detected a musty odor in the upstairs bathroom. A quick search uncovered mold growing in the cabinet under the sink.

I was shocked to realize that for a millisecond I considered not bringing it to Wayne's attention. I quickly regained rationality and called Wayne in to look.

Neither of us detected smells in the rest of the house. Unfortunately, both of us had an irritating sore throat for the rest of the day.

"So what do you think?" I asked Wayne that evening.

"About what?"

"About the cute rent house."

Wayne lowered his notepad and focused his gaze on me. "Carol, you know we can't pursue that house."

I tried to hide the excitement in my voice. "We could remediate the bathroom first. It's the only problem area. The rest of the house was clean, right?" No matter how irrational, I was desperate to return to normalcy; the rope swing outside the charming riverbank home was a siren's call drawing me toward danger. The lure of normalcy and relaxation was overwhelming.

I remembered how excited our young children were when Wayne attached a rope swing to a tall pecan tree in the backyard. They danced from the slide to the teeter-totter to the rope swing and back to the swing set. Our backyard was a child's dream, complete with a sand pile and impossibly thick green grass, making shoes entirely optional from April through September. Our backyard had been magical. *I want some magic back. I'll begin with a rope swing outside a clean house.*

Wayne's eyes flashed defiantly, but his voice remained steady. "Carol, what do you think will happen if we bring mold spores on our shoes or furniture to that house? They already have mold growth. Our mold spores will take over their mold growth, and bam, we are right back where we started, with toxic mold. That house is not an option!"

"You're right, I know." I turned away from his gaze. However irrational, I wanted to pretend we could live there, pretend for a while that we had a solution. I wanted to imagine the kids fishing or catching minnows after school, or taking turns on the rope swing while fireflies danced in the night sky. I wanted our kids to remain in the same schools. I wanted to spend one night imagining a life with clean air, a life not spent fighting mold every day. For one night I wanted to dream about living in the little house in the country.

It turned out Shelby and I were dealing with some of the same feelings. Both of us desperately wanted back in our house and both of us desperately wanted to take a bath.

A few days later, Wayne and I met under a pecan tree to discuss a plan for starting over. Wayne leaned over the patio table. "The only way to stop this is to start over in a completely clean structure. Then only add clean items."

"Right. New items, or items we can clean, like fabric or metal or glass."

Wayne nodded. "Exactly. No leaks or smells or houses we need to fix first. This madness has to stop."

"I agree. It has to stop."

We'd find a spotless, mold-free, odor-free, symptom-free home to buy. We'd look at everything possible in our school district, then expand the search if we had to do so. We would do everything, everything possible, to ensure this never ever happened again.

18

MOLD EXPERT FOR CHRISTMAS

Pam Steward, a microbiologist and the co-founder of ViroTest, arrived at 8:30 p.m. on the Friday before Christmas. She was delayed at a prior testing, but we were relieved she didn't cancel our appointment. We were desperate for her expertise. Pam was petite, and dressed in black jeans and a black T-shirt. Wayne and I followed her through the house babbling questions like first graders. She told us how to build to avoid leaks and mold (use PVC pipe for cold water, copper for hot water, don't put metal braces next to copper lines because they cause pits in the copper lines). When we said we were concerned about mold's impact on our family's health, she said we might benefit from lymphatic drainage, sometimes referred to as "medical massage." She provided contact information for a Houston-based medical massage therapist.

Pam planned to document all areas of the house where leaks had occurred. We started in our bathroom, then walked through every room, pointing out where we'd encountered leaks. Wayne recalled that the dishwasher leaked once. We'd mopped up the water, got a new dishwasher, and moved on with our lives. The kids certainly had lots of fun in the bathtub when they were little and the floor was often wet but we dried it up right away. The kids' toilet overflowed once or twice when they were toddlers, until they learned how much toilet paper was too much. We always cleaned leaks up right away and life went on. We discussed every inch of the house. We pointed and described our leak history as she investigated the areas closely and asked additional questions.

Each time we identified a leak area, Pam asked if there was a "second wetting," which was when the same area got wet during a second, later event.

After living in the house for fifteen years, and not knowing about the original owner's experiences, we answered that yes, the floor around the toilets, tubs, dishwasher, and washing machine had probably been wet more than once.

The den outside Christine's room smelled horrible, which didn't make sense because this was the new part of the house. We had only had one leak—when the remodeling carpenter put a nail through the bathroom water pipe—and that was fixed immediately. There had never been a leak in her bathroom.

I couldn't understand why the new part of the house smelled so terrible without a significant leak. While Pam documented the testing protocol, I asked, "Why does the new part of the house smell worse than the rest of the house ever did? There was only one leak from the nail in the water pipe, and it was fixed immediately. There was no second wetting."

Pam peered over her glasses. "The second wetting must be the humidity."

I stepped forward as my questions spilled quickly. "What? You're telling me we get one chance, *one chance* to have a leak? The *humidity* is enough to cause mold growth after that? The humidity is the second wetting?"

"Yup," she answered matter-of-factly.

It hit me like a lightning bolt—we had to leave this area. There was no grace for the minor spills of life. We had to move away. *We'll never escape the mold while living in this humidity.* Why had no one mentioned this before? If humidity is the second wetting, how did anyone recover from mold here?

When I asked if our house could be fixed, Pam's answer was immediate. "Yes, of course. With proper remediation, your house will pass testing."

I sighed in relief. So while it appeared impossible to me that we could successfully remediate, an expert assured me that we could.

Pam didn't finish our inspection until 11:30 p.m. We thanked her for staying late and answering all our questions.

"Well, you have been through a lot." She shoved her glasses higher on her nose. "I've seen worse, though. Some people sign their insurance check directly over to remediators. The remediators do some work, declare the money gone, then leave the homeowner living in a shell of a house. They don't care—they do it to old people, widows, and families with young children—it doesn't matter. I know families who live in tents outside a moldy house because they have no choice after the insurance money is gone."

I shuddered, imagining children in tents outside a moldy home.

Pam gathered her materials. "Don't forget to fax the information I need, including a floor plan of your house. I'll get the test results back quickly, but not until after the holidays."

Wayne and I felt hopeful after her visit. We learned so much and were thrilled to have a knowledgeable person on our side. Pam told us our house could pass if it was properly remediated. I thought with her expertise we might get our house clean. A few days later, I faxed my meeting notes for her to review.

We didn't go to Maryland for Christmas. My mom had moved to a retirement community, so there wasn't room for us to stay with her. It really didn't matter. We didn't have time to travel. We had plenty keeping us busy in our Texas yard.

Christmas morning in our portable-building bedroom was somber, like one none of us had ever experienced. Our children perched in a semi-circle on the linoleum floor with weak smiles pasted on their faces. Wayne and I leaned forward from the two metal folding chairs to encourage the gift opening process. Plastic file cabinets served as bedside tables and plastic totes held our clothes. We didn't have a Christmas tree or decorations; I couldn't expend energy on items I knew I'd throw in the trash days later.

We paced ourselves through the morning ritual. Wayne and I offered half-hearted observations as they unwrapped their few gifts with remarkable caution and restraint. We'd arrived at a new phase, a "just gut it out" phase. We made the best of our declining situation while figuring out how to climb back to normal.

I have no memory of what gifts they received that morning, but I know most every morning they knew they were loved and knew we tried our best. Years later, I was relieved when the girls said they never worried—and knew we'd take care of them no matter what.

But on that morning, I was devastated that the best I could offer was a meager impermanent-gifting Christmas in our yard, and love-laden promises of a better future.

My awareness that just-opened presents might soon be trashed was gaining real estate in my brain. It was slowly dawning on me that we probably wouldn't keep many items. The RV trailer had mold. The portable-building office had mold, and it was very possible the portable-building bedroom had mold, even though we hadn't stopped trying to clean both buildings. The pattern of losing buildings to mold began with leaks and with contaminated possessions. We had to break free of leaks and contaminated possessions to live in a clean house with clean air.

I knew somehow our lives would go back to normal, or at least to an acceptable version of normal. I knew as well as I'd ever known anything that we'd never spend another Christmas morning on a portable building floor. We had failed to remediate our house. It was a reasonable goal that didn't work. We couldn't and wouldn't keep living like this. We were smart, we had funds, and we had options—we just needed a viable plan. We couldn't beat our mold, but we could stop fighting it. I was finally ready to give up on the fight to save our home.

19

JUST WANT TO DO YOGA

We waited for the kids to leave for school Monday after Christmas break, then cleaned our portable-building bedroom again. Even though we'd cleaned it many times before, the room still made us ill. We had no choice but to keep trying to fix it. We hauled out clothing, shoes, file cabinets, plastic storage boxes, and the folding table and chairs. (We'd moved the offending ash dresser to the garage within a day of first bringing it in, so it had been out for months.) Wayne and I took turns spraying the floor and walls with Consan 20. We hauled everything back in after the chemical dried.

I hardly ran anymore because I felt guilty loping through the neighborhood when I should be cleaning. We needed to get the two travel trailers, the utility van, and the two portable buildings out of our yard. I was sure our neighbors were tired of our mess, a concern that was quickly confirmed. I went for a jog after a particularly difficult day, then met neighbors on an evening walk. The conversation began pleasantly with the typical concerned questions about how we were doing and how long until our house was ready. Then the wife jutted her chin out, crunched her forehead, and offered unsolicited opinions interwoven with pointed questions. She wanted to know why the remediators didn't just clean the mold up, saying she knew of plenty of people who had recovered from mold. She repeatedly insisted they should finish cleaning so we could move back in our house. Stunned, all I could do was nod in agreement. After all, I wanted the same damn thing, every day, all day long. Her husband studied the asphalt and shifted his weight until it became clear she could not stop herself from badgering me. He finally intervened, "They are doing all they can; stop asking her why their house isn't clean!" He tugged on her arm and she reluctantly followed, still sputtering and asking me why our house wasn't clean yet. Left more stressed than when I began, I avoided jogging from then on.

The lack of understanding made our experience very lonely. People told us we were paranoid and overreacting; that mold was everywhere and you could never get away from it. One man insisted that as soon as insurance companies stopped covering mold remediation, the mold contamination stories would cease as well. Many people asked why the cleanup was taking so long. Friends told us mold didn't bother them, that it was all in our heads. It was disheartening, even though I'd been warned people wouldn't understand. It was discouraging to suffer through our experience while being discounted as overreacting or paranoid. Wayne and I talked about it, and wondered if someone's house burned down, would his neighbors tell him he was paranoid or it was all in his head? Of course not, they'd offer sympathy and assistance, not disbelief. Most people didn't understand mold contamination and the lengthy, difficult clean-up process, or the vast health ramifications. Several times Wayne said it would have been easier if our house burned. We would have moved on and rebuilt our lives. But burning the house wasn't an option; the insurance company was clear about that. Instead, we were stuck in smelly sickening limbo.

Thank goodness our families were supportive. My mom was always available to listen, always sympathetic and confident we were doing the right thing. Wayne's parents never questioned our situation or the mold, and always welcomed us to their home as a place to recharge, which was extremely kind. My mom's willingness to listen—and my in-laws' willingness to host us—provided me with hope that carried me through the tough times.

Many friends were supportive, especially once they had more information, but most had their own lives overscheduled with soccer, football, dance, and other activities. Over time, Wayne and I found it difficult to talk about our experience with much control. We had a hard time answering a simple question, such as "How did the mold start?" or "How many remediations have you had?" without providing excessive detail. We found it difficult to stop our recitation once we started telling the story. While we knew our reactions were inappropriate, we had trouble controlling our narrative. We finally started answering with a noncommittal "It's fine," or "Making progress," or a similar comment to avoid our kneejerk accounting. Between our busy schedule, our extreme preoccupation with mold remediation, and my pathetic caged-animal mannerisms, it was not a friendship-building time in our lives.

We were ecstatic when a beautiful home in our neighborhood was listed for sale. It was perfect—two stories of hardwood and tile, high ceilings, four bedrooms, and a gorgeous yard. While expensive, it was the perfect solution, so we quickly negotiated a price. None of us noticed an odor or had allergic reactions, so we were sure it was clean enough.

We finally found a solution.

We'd have to be very careful when bringing possessions to this clean, airy home, but felt up to the task. During the leisurely final walk-through, I felt like the home's title had already been transferred as I relaxed against doorjambs, peered inside airy closets, and trailed my hand along dark granite countertops. Wayne and I waited in the three-car garage while the realtor locked up.

Perhaps I didn't want to leave yet, perhaps I still wanted to touch more surfaces, but for some reason I walked into the garage bathroom, lifted the lid of the toilet tank, and found black mold growing underneath the lid. I immediately showed Wayne—not for a millisecond did I consider otherwise—and we quickly left. Later that night, Wayne told the realtor we wouldn't go forward with the purchase and they could keep our earnest money. The realtor tried to talk Wayne out of it, saying a little bit of mildew on the garage bathroom toilet tank lid wasn't a big deal. He was right, it wasn't a big deal to most people, but it was a very big deal to us. We didn't want to forfeit the money—this was totally out of character for both of us—but Wayne and I were solidly on the same page. We would not purchase a house with visible mold growth.

I was desperate to find a way to exercise outside of public view. I bought a yoga video during Christmas break and tried again in the girls' trailer, but of course there still wasn't enough floor space. Again, I was more stressed after my exercise attempt than I was before I started.

Wayne knew exercise was critical to my well-being and was determined to honor my request for yoga. Exercise kept me in the ranks of non-suicidal, non-caustic, reasonably patient folks. The remediators had delivered our cleaned VCR and TV a month before. Wayne cleaned them again in the garage and set them up in our portable building bedroom. The TV was off, but he was adjusting the VCR when I stepped up into the bedroom. I immediately felt an extremely sharp pain in my ears, like someone forcibly slammed cupped hands against my ears.

"Oh my God, Wayne! Get that VCR out of here! My ears hurt bad!" I wiped my nose, which had immediately started flowing.

"What? Okay; I'll get it out of here." Wayne pushed the power button and unplugged the VCR. "I don't get it. They cleaned it, and I cleaned it again. I guess I'll clean it again."

After that, I suffered from sharp, painful earaches and a stuffy nose after being in the bedroom. Wayne had a stuffy nose as well. We continued trying to fix the bedroom so we could sleep there.

Wayne thought we might be reacting to the dry-cleaning chemicals, so he decided we should remove our hanging clothes. All we could do was clean and remove items until we stopped reacting to our bedroom. We packed necessary clothes and shoes in plastic bins, and stored the rest in the utility trailer. We removed file cabinets, folding table, and chairs; everything we could move was moved. Then we sprayed the floor and walls with Consan 20. This effort improved our reactions to the bedroom.

The next evening, I left the kids doing homework in the trailer after dinner. I was excited to hear the TV news as I walked toward our bedroom. I hadn't watched the news in well over a year, and the announcer's tone indicated an exciting report. Wayne said he'd clean, then test the TV in the open garage before bringing it inside. I was excited that apparently his garage test was successful. I opened the portable building door, then saw Wayne slouched in a folding chair with the TV blaring in the middle of the floor.

I immediately yelled, "Shit, Wayne!"

"Hmm?" He slowly turned to me, a vacant look on his face.

"My head is pounding! Whatever's in that TV gave me a headache as soon as I walked in. Didn't you notice? We have to get it out of here!" I punched off the power button, then turned toward him.

He didn't move except to slowly lift his head toward me. Stunned by the empty look in his eyes, I realized he was incapacitated. I didn't know how long he'd been in the room with that TV, but he wasn't functioning now.

I quickly unplugged the TV, then gingerly touched his elbow to coax him up. "Come on, honey. Grab the other end of the TV because I can't lift this myself."

My brilliant husband obeyed like a dutiful child as we carried the contaminated TV outside.

I was shocked and frightened as the enormity of the situation sunk in. Clearly, our TV and VCR had not been professionally cleaned, as the remediators had promised during contract signing. Neither Wayne nor I could fathom such behavior, that a firm would agree and collect payment for work, then never do it. The fact that they'd return contaminated possessions to us was unbelievable.

Even more shocking, it was clear our possessions were contaminated with mold from other remediation customers while stored in the Houston warehouse. I never got an immediate, stabbing headache, or had my nose run uncontrollably in our old house. I never felt like someone slammed their palms against my ears in our old house. These new reactions were due to mold that hadn't been in our house. Our mold foe had become stronger, and our partner in the fight—our remediators—was helping the mold win.

NEED TO TELL YOU SOMETHING

I was excited to schedule testing with two firms and the remediation firm on a Saturday in mid-January. Cancellation was unlikely because the insurance company would be upset if testing wasn't conducted simultaneously by both firms. We'd come a long way from enduring radio silence from Friday till Monday. After suffering through months of unanswered calls and repeated cancellations, it was a huge relief to finally get the attention necessary to make progress. We needed accurate test results to move forward.

Rain was forecast for Saturday, so I checked with our testing company to ensure weather wouldn't be a problem. False positives are more likely when air samples are conducted during rainy weather. We'd had air sample testing cancelled because samples were affected by current levels of rain, humidity, and weather changes. I was relieved when Liz, Pam's assistant, assured me weather wouldn't delay testing because they were only conducting tape samples. I was ecstatic because I'd read that tape samples were more reliable than air samples.

There was another reason I was thrilled they'd only collect

tape samples. I knew disreputable remediators sprayed chemicals to hold mold particles down along the floor prior to testing. Air samples are gathered three to six feet off the ground, so this procedure limited mold detection via air sampling. It was possible that our remediators utilized this trick prior to our December testing, which explained why the air samples didn't confirm mold. After all, I'd learned about the trick from Steve last year when he described how unethical firms ensured a house passed testing.

Pam and Liz arrived Saturday afternoon to collect tape samples of areas targeted during our prior meeting. Kelly from TESTX arrived thirty minutes later and began testing for our insurance company. I was certain our house wouldn't pass. In some ways, our reactions to our home's mold were stronger than when we were first ordered to evacuate. Still, I was nervous. I didn't know what would happen if the insurance company results showed the house passed but Pam's results showed it failed.

TESTX finished after several hours, while Liz and Pam continued testing. I found Pam and Liz in the living room around 5:30 p.m. While talking, I noticed a black circle slightly larger than a quarter on the rock fireplace behind them. I'd looked at that fireplace for sixteen years and the circle looked strange. I walked over for a closer look. "Hey guys, I think there's mold growing on the fireplace."

Pam examined the spot, then asked Liz to gather samples of the black mold. Liz pulled tape from her test kit.

I shook my head in disbelief. Even though it was a small spot, it was more than what existed when we first moved out. We didn't have any visible mold growth when we evacuated a year ago last October. "I can't believe, after all the time and money spent, we have mold actually growing on the fireplace!

It's worse than ever in here!"

That evening we unfolded three camping chairs in front of the garage. Wayne and I vented to Pam about our evolving bedroom mold problems while we shared a pizza.

"I can't believe CleanHome didn't clean our possessions," Wayne began. "Our bedroom is contaminated with our original mold, plus now we have Houston's mold growing there as well."

"Exactly," I chimed in. "The original mold from our house made us stupid. Now I get severe headaches, stabbing earaches, and a runny nose that won't quit in the portable building. I didn't have those reactions in our old house. Now we have new mold to deal with. I can't believe it, it just gets worse."

Maybe it was the carbohydrates, or the way we clung to her every word, or the late hour, but Pam's professional guard lifted. She took a deep breath. "I need to tell you something. You have to find different remediators. CleanHome are crooks."

"What do you mean?" Wayne asked.

"They declared bankruptcy six months ago. They are crooks. The owner declares bankruptcy and reopens a new company under someone else's name so he can't be traced."

"I *knew* it. They insisted Carol write the check to a new company last month. So, they're defrauding their creditors right now," Wayne said.

"The owner is a real shit. They finally got him, though. He's going to prison for fraud and income tax evasion." Pam took a sip of water.

"Prison; I can't believe it! After my months of research and checking, how did I end up with such a low-life remediation firm?" I wondered.

"Hey, it's not your fault. There was no way for you to know. None of the had reviews, bankruptcies, or liens were tied to him. When he gets into trouble, he opens a new firm with a new name and new owners so he can't be traced." Pam frowned. "He used all his family members, so the new firm is in his secretary's name. She probably agreed to save her job. He keeps clients by lying to them, like with you. You didn't know the firm went bankrupt six months ago."

"Right, we didn't know any of this. We never met the owner, but his son is truly evil. I've never said that about anyone." I felt the hair stand up on my neck when I remembered Gordon's only visit.

Pam said we needed to find someone else to clean our house. "I just feel so sorry for you guys."

She must have shared more than planned, because then she rose from her chair. "Listen, it's really late. I'll get your test results to you as soon as I can. Take care."

Wayne and I watched her drive away as we sat in our dark garage and wondered what to do next. Our house was contaminated. All our possessions were contaminated, more contaminated than they were sixteen months ago. Our house, office, bedroom, big trailer, and utility trailer were contaminated as well. Our remediators were crooks and the owner was going to prison. We had to figure a way out of this mess.

THAT'S SMOOTH

Wayne and I spent Sunday in a daze. We were shocked that CleanHome declared bankruptcy six months ago, and the owner was headed for prison. We were sick that our possessions were more contaminated than when they left our toxic home. We had no reason to hope that our remediation firm—newly named Spotless Inc.—would ever rid our house of toxic mold.

Wayne was adamant about not paying Spotless Inc. since we didn't have a contract with them. He said they defrauded their creditors by operating under a new name and collecting money from CleanHome's customers. "We won't pay them another dime. Once they realize we won't pay more, they won't let us have our items back. We need our belongings back. We paid for cleaning and storage and we need them back."

I panicked at the thought of receiving contaminated contents. "But our items are contaminated! The TV and VCR ruined our bedroom." I could feel my pulse racing. "I don't want moldy things back. We're barely making it now." My voice cracked. I'd had enough of contaminated items.

"I agree. But some things can be cleaned. I want the artwork back, so tell Steve to return it. It's framed to museum quality with a glass front. We can pull off the backing and have the art reframed."

I nodded while I tried to find common ground with my husband. "Yes, some items can be cleaned. Dishes, china, metal, and glass. All those can be cleaned."

We created a plan of action: 1) find a new remediation company, 2) get information about the bankruptcy proceedings and charges against the owner, 3) find out how to clean our possessions and what can/can't be cleaned, 4) share this information with our adjuster and get his input, 5) get important items returned before Spotless Inc. discovers we know they are crooks and stops working with us, and 6) contact a lawyer because we probably needed one.

I tried to called Steve, but all the remediation company phone numbers were disconnected. I finally got his new number a few days later. I told him Pam had completed the additional testing. I tried to keep the conversation light. I asked for his build back plan so we could prepare for the next step. I mentioned I'd faxed a list of contents we needed returned.

The next day we received a $50,000 invoice from Spotless Inc. for machine rental and storing our contents since November. Heat radiated from my forehead across my scalp.

I left a lengthy message for our adjuster, "Kevin, we got a huge bill from Spotless Inc. for renting the dehumidifiers and negative air machines, and for storing our belongings. They can't do this, right? These charges were included—and paid for—in each remediation plan. They can't create invoices out of thin air, right?"

I located CleanHome's bankruptcy information online. They filed for bankruptcy in the summer of 2003. *Now I knew why they didn't answer my calls for six weeks.* They had numerous lawsuits, liens, and judgments against them. I started chastising myself for missing this information, but the claims were against companies with other names and other owners, so as Pam said, I couldn't have known. When the lawsuits and negative reviews became too much, they closed the company and opened under a new name with a new owner—no past failings were tied to the new company.

After being ordered to evacuate, I'd spent months collecting information about remediators under pressure that the longer I searched, the more contaminated our house would become in the heat and humidity. I'd gathered all the information I could, then we made a choice. Sixteen months later it was clearly the wrong choice, but I didn't fault my efforts. They'd lied to us since the very beginning.

I called Liz at the testing firm to find out what experts believed could be cleaned, and what should be thrown out. She said to trash pillows, wicker furniture, books, stuffed animals, and mattresses. The "maybe" category included wool blend rugs, leather items, and wood furniture. She provided the name of an art restoration company that cleaned artwork. She said we could triple HEPA filter and then use leather cleaner on leather furniture, but test it before bringing it to a clean location. Wood furniture could usually be cleaned if all surfaces were sealed or painted. She said don't keep unsealed wood (even drawers), and don't keep any furniture containing particle board. While disappointed that unsealed wood wasn't acceptable, I was glad to have the information. I had to know what wasn't cleanable so we didn't bring mold to our next home. No matter how hard it was to hear, I needed the information.

Wayne and I struggled with how to deal with Spotless: the

ridiculous bill, contaminated contents, unlivable house, and bankruptcy. We didn't want or need more drama, but drama had found us. We decided to contact a lawyer. We wanted our possessions back—at least possessions that could be cleaned. We were willing to pay what was owed less offsets due to missing, contaminated, or damaged belongings. But we wouldn't pay $50,000 for work we'd already paid for.

Wayne continued his epic fight to clean our portable-building bedroom. He sprayed the entire room with Consan 20 repeatedly. Each time the two of us had to remove everything (clothes, bed, toiletries, plastic bins, etc.) to coat the floor, walls, and ceiling. The air was cleaner for a few days, then became heavy, then became bad again. He sprayed the newly purchased window AC/heater unit, which provided a few days of relief as well.

I wasn't sure how much more stress I could take. I had visions of stripping naked and plodding down the street until being picked up by hospital staff. It was always hospital staff, so even in my darkest moments I harbored a tiny bit of hope that things would get better. The staff deposited me at a mold-free mental ward with clean air, where I lounged in the sunny TV room and didn't worry about outrageous bills from criminal remediators. I knew I could get away from the mold; all I had to do was start driving or walking. But those were fantasies of a stress-addled brain. I'd never leave Wayne and the kids, and it was unimaginable that I'd purposefully leave my spouse to deal with this alone. We couldn't make it out of this mess without the effort of two functioning adults. Checking out or leaving were not options. Now was not the time to develop a drinking problem, sleep all day, or engage in other inappropriate coping mechanisms.

I noticed Wayne was becoming more irritable with me and the kids. It was understandable because of the extreme stress, but it wasn't like him. He never sang anymore and hardly joked or teased us either. I wasn't sure how much more he could take. He had been on antidepressants for years and I didn't know if a dosage increase would even solve this. He had every right to be depressed, but what would happen if he actually stopped coping?

When I asked how he was doing, he said he was okay, not great. Then he added, "Every morning when I wake my first thought is, 'What in the hell do I have to clean today?'"

"We really should have bought stock in Clorox!"

"Damn right. When I die, I want you to bury me clutching a Clorox Clean-Up bottle in my hand because that's all I do is spray stuff, all day, every day," he grinned.

I felt better, but was still worried. Wayne was right, all he did was clean things and spray things day after day. He never stopped and never gave up. But he did suffer from depression, and there was no guarantee he would be able to keep going, that he wouldn't give up. I knew as long as he could function, he'd never leave us. As long as he could function, he would keep me informed; we had always talked about our thoughts, feelings, and plans. Still, I worried because I didn't know how much more he could take, whether our situation, coupled with his depression, could cause him to give up.

I remember when clinical depression led my dad to sit in a rocking chair and chain-smoke Pall Malls all day. I tried to sneak down the stairs and leave for fourth grade without him noticing, but his vacant eyes managed to locate me through the smoke. Clearly, he was miles away and his disappearance— while physically present—irritated me to no end. My mom said therapy was a slow process, but he would eventually get better. My parents did the best they could since antidepressant medications weren't available in the mid-sixties. But the smoke and his hairy legs sticking out from his nightshirt commandeered our living room for too long. Dad recovered after two years, but that was a confusing and frightening time for me.

That episode provided me with a critical life lesson: Shit can happen to anyone, anytime, and sometimes you can't see or understand it, much less fix it. I had no reason to believe Wayne would disappear into a rocking chair, except I'd seen it happen under much less stressful circumstances. Once again, I was frightened, and my fear was valid. It was possible the stress would become too much and Wayne would just check out. I worried more than usual, which didn't seem possible given my normal worry volume. I couldn't lose Wayne; I couldn't handle this without his help.

Wayne and I prepped for the next call from Spotless Inc. Wayne's job was to stay cool and say what was necessary to keep the relationship positive. We wanted our belongings returned to a neutral location before our connection with Spotless totally deteriorated. We wouldn't divulge that we knew they'd declared bankruptcy, but would focus on getting our possessions back. Wayne and I weren't in total agreement about whether we could get our contents clean. He was more positive than I was on that point, but at a minimum he wanted the artwork returned. We agreed that he'd pursue getting our items returned while I'd research what classes of items could be remediated and which should be trashed.

I felt Wayne's irritation as soon as I stepped up to our office and heard him on the call. He was breathing heavily as he hunched over his desk and stared at the speaker phone.

Wayne said, "I never signed a contract with Spotless Inc. So how did they get my possessions?"

Gordon responded flatly, "I can't answer that."

Wayne tapped his pen against the desk. "That TV and VCR you returned to us contaminated our new $10,000 portable building and the AC unit. That building is ruined; we can't sleep there without opening the windows. Are you going to pay to replace that?"

Gordon said he couldn't answer that either.

Wayne's frown deepened. "You proved you can't clean my belongings. I sure as hell don't want them back." Gordon insisted we wanted our belongings back. He said we had to want our piano, antiques, china, furniture, electronics, and artwork returned—all we had to do was pay $50,000.

Wayne's voice lowered as he leaned forward. "I'd be crazy to take our possessions back, after what happened. That TV and VCR infected our bedroom with toxic mold; they'll infect any house we move to. Why would I want contaminated items back?"

After a long silence, Gordon replied, "Well, you have my number, Mr. Milberger."

Wayne's hands gripped the edge of the desk as he yelled, "Yeah, I got your number, and it's fuckin' zero!" He punched off the speaker phone and collapsed back in his chair.

Our plan of action, our strategy, was abandoned in mere minutes. Instead of playing it cool, Wayne had argued with Gordon about the absurd additional charges. I narrowed my eyes to bring the events into focus. I didn't fault Wayne; Gordon's demands were ridiculous. But it was a bit absurd, even comical, to hear how far the conversation strayed from our carefully constructed plan.

I grinned. "Well, that didn't go as we planned."

Wayne provided a weak grin in response. "I'm sorry. I tried, but I couldn't do it. He began the call by demanding $50,000 for our contaminated items—when we'd already paid for cleaning and storing those items! The whole thing is ridiculous. I couldn't pretend everything was fine, because it's not. I couldn't do it, because it's crazy."

Wayne stared at the far wall. "I guess it went downhill from there. You heard the rest."

"Way to play it cool." I couldn't help but tease him. The phone call wasn't close to what we planned, but most of our current life wasn't what we'd planned. Much of the cleaning and our efforts now felt pointless, like bailing water from a sinking boat. But we had to keep trying, no matter what. We planned and executed, then made adjustments, while trying to adjust to rapid changes. But when it got too ridiculous, we occasionally threw up our hands, teased and laughed, then got back to work.

Wayne looked at me. "Gordon said he'll get the money from our insurance company if we don't pay. We need to make sure the insurance company doesn't pay him."

"I'll tell our adjuster the invoice is bogus and we already paid for cleaning and storage. Plus, they didn't clean our items or store them correctly." I walked toward my office, then turned back to Wayne. "We'll get through this, right? It's crazy, but we can do it."

"Of course we will. It's just senseless that we have to fight the remediators in addition to the mold. We have enough to do already. But we can do it." Wayne grabbed his pen, and I turned to my office to make a call. Our lawyer sent the remediators a demand letter stating we didn't have a contract with Spotless Inc. We demanded they deliver our possessions to a new storage unit where we would conduct an inventory and have items tested. We offered to pay the original company what was owed, deducting costs for missing, damaged, or contaminated contents. Gordon refused our demands. He reiterated that they wouldn't return any of our possessions until we paid the new company $50,000.

22

A CLEAN PLACE TO SLEEP

Wayne, Justin, and I visited a house for sale in a nearby neighborhood in February. It was painfully small and in a different school district. I had no idea how we'd fit, much less work from there. But it was clean, so we reluctantly began to work through the purchase process. We had to get to a clean place.

Our bedroom continued to deteriorate. We couldn't fix it, even though we spent a tremendous amount of time trying. Wayne cleaned it countless times, and cleaned the AC/heater window unit as well. Every time I walked in, I got a severe stuffy nose right away. After a while it got so bad it was almost impossible to breathe, so of course I couldn't sleep. Wayne finally pushed out the AC/heater to the ground below, then covered the hole with plastic sheeting. We followed with our normal routine of spraying, mopping, then wiping down the walls. The room smelled much better, and I was relieved to be able to breathe and sleep. It was cold at night without a heater. I wondered how long the AC unit would lie on the lawn. Ruined appliances left on the lawn was uncharted territory for us.

Wayne thought paint might seal in the mold, so two days later we painted. I was sick of trying to fix the unfixable, but had to support my husband's goal to make things better. We removed everything except the bed and plastic boxes. We threw away our shoes and bought new ones. Wayne sprayed the entire room, and we wiped down the floor, walls, and everything else. Over the next few days, we painted the walls, floor, and ceiling, hoping paint would seal in the mold. I was unenthusiastic, sluggishly dragging paint across the wall, it was absurd. I wanted to be anywhere but wielding a paint brush in that moldy portable building. Even though I was exhausted, I also harbored hope that painting would make the bedroom bearable.

All the repeated effort didn't make sense. It seemed as if no matter what we did, the outcome was still bad. We were caught in a merry-go-round of futile efforts. We cleaned, then the mold's effects returned. Effort was pointless as the mold overtook our solutions, but doing nothing was more pointless. When I came face-to-face with the futility of our efforts coupled with our inability to stop, I found it irrational and depressing.

Wayne kept at it though. A few days later, he sprayed the office and then we wiped everything down. The office wasn't too terribly bad, at least in my opinion. It gave me a sore throat, but I just dealt with it, it was doable for me. Wayne, however, didn't like the office at all. He insisted he couldn't think there, so I hoped cleaning would help.

After five months of sleeping in a portable building, Wayne finally hooked up the hot water heater. I stood at the sink and let warm water flow, warming my hands as I rubbed them with soap. My face felt so clean after washing, I was a new person, and almost human, when I got into bed that night.

Ever since last fall, we'd tried to get the big RV clean enough to live in. We cleaned it numerous times and aired it out, but weren't successful. The RV dealer that cleaned it offered to sell it as well, so we finally decided to do so—we needed to move it out of the backyard. A few days later Wayne pulled the big RV back to the Houston dealer. We felt bad about selling it, but could only handle one disaster at a time. The dealer said it was clean, and we'd paid dearly for that cleaning. Plus, sometimes we wondered if we'd become overly sensitive to smells after all we'd been through. Dust made us nervous and the thought of mold made us cringe.

Christine had a screening interview at her top university choice. We spent several evenings doing practice interviews with questions I created. Between our practice interviews and Christine's debate training, I knew she'd interview well.

We drove to Houston. I sat on a campus bench to people-watch in the sun during her interview. Finally, I saw her walk towards me.

"How did it go?" I asked, excitedly.

"It went really well," she responded. "He said he's never seen such a packed resume! He asked how I had time to sleep during high school!"

"That's wonderful! You know they get tons of impressive resumes, so all your hard work paid off!" I was so excited the interview went well. It was wonderful to have positive news in our lives.

Christine smiled broadly; she was clearly thrilled. We celebrated with a leisurely lunch at an upscale West University restaurant. We talked about how fun and interesting college would be, that she could take courses in anything that interested her. We lunched and forgot about toxic mold.

I was glad we had a fun visit, because I was horrible to her a week later. Somewhere in the mold ordeal timeline, I developed an extreme aversion to damp air. The greater the humidity, the deeper my transformation. In a heavy mist, my shoulders hunched forward and my chin tucked down while I furtively scanned the horizon for threats. I was overwhelmed as mold grew, unchecked, around me. I was trapped, and I was angry.

My mood was evident when Christine asked if her band friends could practice at our house on a rainy Saturday. "No, they can't come over; we don't even have a house," I barked. I was livid, watching rain gush off the garage roof and pound patterns on the driveway. Our mold had flourished in less humidity. I angrily paced the thick, misty cage of our garage.

This was a far cry from the mom I used to be; I had practically lived for my children's friends to visit. I'd provided meals, snacks, crafts, and movies, and I'd endured overnights.

Christine searched my face for clues about her misplaced mom. "We'll practice in the garage."

Furious, I snapped, "Couldn't you go to someone's house that *doesn't* have toxic mold? Come on, Christine; out of nine families, how is it possible that our garage, surrounded by two portable buildings, travel trailers, and a utility van outside a moldy house is the best place to hold band practice?" I waved my hands in the direction of all our failures.

An inappropriate response to my daughter's grasp at normal life, but the idea of kids gathered in a possibly moldy garage surrounded by rain pissed me off. I could smell the mold in the wet, humid air, and it infuriated me. I didn't want kids, or their instruments, in our garage. Especially trumpet players with those ridiculous spit valves. I was introduced to trumpet spit valves when Justin began playing a few years ago. What if a mold spore landed in the spit valve, then was locked in the case for a week?

Christine held her ground. "Mom, none of them have room, so it has to be here. I already told them to come over."

I realized the rain angered me, and if compliant Christine wouldn't budge, then I was definitely being unreasonable. I shoved back my fury and agreed she could host her friends, but insisted the overhead garage doors remain open for ventilation.

Unfortunately, I had to walk past their sweep of camp chairs to access my sanity-saving-place, my office. Maintaining a forced smile robbed oxygen from my arms and legs, resulting in a rigid, disjointed advance across wet pavement. I grinned at their general direction while my eyes and body screamed, *Run away while you still can.*

23

WHO'S IN JAIL?

Wayne began talking as soon as he stepped in the girls' trailer for lunch. "You're not going to believe what I found out! Remember Clinton, the owner of the dry-cleaning company we used? I told you we've been talking."

I nodded as Wayne continued, "Well, CleanHome refused to reimburse Clinton $67,000 for doing dry-cleaning work. $67,000 of dry cleaning! Clinton sued CleanHome and the owner, Matt Hawk, but Clinton somehow lost the suit."

I brought vegetable beef soup to the table and sat across from Wayne. I wasn't surprised; no one could win against Hawk. He lied more than he told the truth.

"Guess what else? Hawk is *already* in prison for tax evasion! He didn't pay taxes when he opened and closed companies under different names and owners. Clinton said he and other creditors attended the bankruptcy hearing. Clinton was furious; he said Hawk was tan and sporting a golf shirt, like he'd stopped on his way to a country club lunch. The creditors are spitting mad."

I nodded. So, the owner of our remediation company was already in prison.

"Guess what else? All the moldy possessions are stored in one big room!"

Incredulous, I put my spoon down. "Oh, come on; that's not possible! It isn't stored in separate rooms like they promised? All those moldy couches, rugs, art, drapes, tables, toys, and electronics are stored in one big room? That's criminal! No wonder our stuff came back with everyone else's mold!"

"Wait, there's more. The room isn't even climate controlled! They can't control humidity without climate control!"

I shook my head in utter disbelief, shocked at the news. "No air-conditioning, as guaranteed? Mold grows like crazy in Houston's humidity, just like it did here!" I had absolutely no experience with such a situation; none at all. "The contract said the facility was climate-controlled. It stated our items would be stored in separate rooms, away from contents of other mold clients. They didn't honor a signed contract!"

"Wait, wait! That's not all," Wayne said excitedly. "Since they are in bankruptcy, our possessions are locked up. No one can get to them, especially CleanHome. Gordon was lying when he said he'd deliver our contents if we paid them. He can't even get in the building to get our contents!"

I smiled, relieved to clearly glimpse who we'd been dealing with. Even until the very end Gordon lied, and lied big. We'd been dealing with liars and cheats. I had trouble fathoming such people existed. We had not selected a reputable firm.

I asked Wayne why the dry cleaner relied on remediators instead of clients for payment. Wayne said remediators often convinced clients to direct payments to the remediation firm and the firm would "take care of everything." Overwhelmed clients often agreed and then didn't have leverage on how their money was spent. This also led to firms, like dry cleaners, not getting paid for their work. When CleanHome stopped paying customers' bills, Clinton's company couldn't collect.

After waiting two long months for test results, I received a call from the insurance company home office. I held my breath while the manager relayed the insurance company's independent test results, that our house *still* had toxic mold.

The manager added, "You are at the end of your insured amount. There isn't enough insurance money to finish cleaning and rebuilding your house." He paused, then added, "We've decided to award you the balance of your insurance money. It is your choice whether you want to continue cleaning your house."

I exhaled in relief. Finally, we had control over how the insurance money was spent. We didn't have to keep trying to clean a house that didn't appear to be cleanable. After all this time, it finally was our choice.

The manager ended the call by saying, "This is your money. How you deal with CleanHome is your business."

I leaned forward to rest my head on the desk.

After seventeen months, we still had toxic mold. But now we controlled our insurance money and the cleaning process. I didn't blame the insurance company for trying to manage how our insurance money was spent; it was natural to try to control costs. But their management drew the process out. Their management hampered our ability to make appropriate choices and clean the house the first time. I'm sure many clients needed cost-management, but Wayne and I needed mold remediation expertise, not cost-management. Now that there wasn't enough money left to fix the house, they were done with the project. Well, we were done as well. We'd been done for a long, long time.

After Justin complained that his ear hurt from sleeping in the office, Wayne folded up the kitchen table and laid cushions down to create a second twin bed in the girls' trailer. Now it really looked like a dorm room. Shelby's bed was directly in front of the door, and remained a muddle of books, pillows, jeans, shirts, socks, sheets, and a comforter. Justin's unmade bed bumped up to the left of Shelby's. The wall across from their beds hosted the sink, refrigerator, stove, oven, and bathroom. Christine's room was past the bathroom and Justin's bed.

The kids stuffed their belongings into cabinets above and below their beds. Christine's debate suits, along with the girls' dresses and blouses, were crammed in two tiny closets on either side of her bed. The term "dorm room décor" described the lifestyle we'd fallen into. The kids wore the same clothing over and over. Admittedly, they wore jeans without washing them when we lived in our house, but now, without storage options, they were professional laundry-avoiders. Their bedtime ritual included draping their jeans along the base of the bed before slipping on an oversized T-shirt. The next morning they'd slide into waiting jeans and pull on a new shirt. I assumed they changed underwear.

Their beds became couches and eating areas during the day. We simply pushed the comforter over and plopped down to eat. When the weather was nice, we sometimes ate dinner at our iron patio set under the tall pecan trees. It was pleasant to dine al fresco some evenings.

We shared the same tiny bathroom in the girls' trailer. I still don't know how Wayne managed to turn around in the miniature shower. He said it wasn't an issue, but I wondered if he washed his front and back on alternate days to avoid negotiating the tiny space.

The kids did their homework while sitting in bed. Two years earlier, I would have insisted they do their homework at a desk or the kitchen table, since sitting on a bed wasn't suitable for their posture or eyes. Eating dinner in bed would have been unthinkable, it wouldn't have entered our minds as a possibility.

Christine's bedroom at the back of the trailer had an accordion fabric door at the base of the bed. She pulled the accordion door shut each evening so the light wouldn't bother her siblings while she studied late. Meow Meow was always invited, and served as her cheerleader and companion during the late-night sessions. He curled up next to her and winked, stretched, and yawned his support into the wee hours of the night. She told me he was a top-notch listener as well, nodding at the right moments and providing quiet time for her to reflect. She confided that Meow Meow looked like a wise old man with his comforting, half-closed gaze. Years later, she insisted she wouldn't have been able to study so late without Meow Meow's steady companionship.

Christine and I finally managed to escape to visit her backup college choices in Austin and San Antonio. I was thrilled to finally do my part as a "good" mom and take her on campus visits. She was slated to graduate as valedictorian. The top 10 percent of every class was guaranteed acceptance at all state universities. That didn't guarantee acceptance to her desired major, but we were confident she'd get in.

I was ecstatic to have a weekend away from our failing home life. I felt like royalty, relishing the Hampton Inn's clean sheets, spacious bathroom, and clean air. A five-star hotel would have caused cardiac arrest. Beyond thrilled with our accommodations, I never wanted to leave. I stayed present with Christine. I didn't think about returning to our moldy surroundings. I didn't think about cleaning buildings over and over. I avoided worrying whether we'd be able to clean the office and bedroom enough for us to live and work there. No matter what happened,

Christine would move to a mold-free dorm in August.

Ever since Pam, the expert tester, told me that humidity is "…the second wetting," I'd been adamant about moving to a drier climate. I searched online for houses in several small towns in the Texas Hill Country north of San Antonio and west of Austin. I found several beautiful small towns with low humidity. I became convinced that this was the solution, to move to a place with low humidity. As far as I was concerned, low humidity equaled grace, and grace meant, in our case, adequate time to fix the inevitable leaks of normal life.

Wayne and I had visited the town of Pleasant Hills many times while taking the kids to summer camp. Besides the weather, we loved the beautiful hills, the river, and the variety of activities available in a fairly small town. We had discussed moving to Pleasant Hills as a solution, but I wasn't certain Wayne would leave his family and the farm.

I asked Wayne if we could talk one afternoon before the kids returned from school. I was nervous as we sat under the shade of a pecan tree—I wanted to move away to start over and wasn't sure he did. I leaned forward, "We know the only way to safely start over is to move to a drier climate. Anita from church moved to Pleasant Hills. She said their average low humidity is in the forties versus our average low in the sixties. No matter how careful we are, we're bound to bring some mold spores with us when we move, so it needs to be so dry they can't flourish. We simply cannot contaminate the next house; we wouldn't survive it."

Wayne remained quiet, then finally spoke. "There is no way I can go through this again. I can't. I'm not even sure I can continue now."

"We've talked about it before, but could you move to the Hill

Country?" I could hear the hope in my voice. "Could you stand being that far away from the farms, the ranch, and your family?"

"It might be our best option. We've looked at houses here and haven't found anything; and some of them have mold." Wayne paused, then said, "We might have to escape the humidity to start over."

I felt my heart pound. "Wayne, that's awesome! I know it's the right thing to do! It's much drier up there, so we have a better chance of starting over without contamination, don't you think?"

Wayne nodded and smiled slightly.

"But land is too expensive to ranch or farm there. I'll keep consulting and drive to Houston for meetings." I paused, then asked, "What will you do?"

"I don't know, but I'll figure it out. It will take time to get rid of this house and the buildings. Then I'll figure out what's next." He looked up and grinned, "Maybe I'll do nothing for a while."

I beamed, then relaxed back in the patio chair. "Imagine doing nothing; how wonderful! Sleep, get up, and manage the kids. No cleaning, no spraying, no dealing with crooked remediators, insurance, or lawsuits."

I watched a tree branch sway in the breeze. "I wish we didn't have to move them; it's so tough to start over at these ages. At least they'll be in good schools with lots of activities. I hope they adjust."

Wayne countered, "We did everything, everything possible to keep from moving them. It didn't work. They know we tried. They'll adjust."

"I hope you are right. We did everything we could to stay here, that is for sure." I looked up at Wayne and brightened. "I'm so excited we're doing this! We can visit on weekends to see houses. I can't wait!"

I was surprised, but thrilled that Wayne said he'd move. I had trouble imagining a farmer/rancher without a farm or a ranch, though. He'd visit the farm as needed, since it was just a five-hour drive, but this would be a huge adjustment. But we couldn't go on like this. In order to start over we had to get away from the humidity.

Wayne hated our portable-building office now. He felt terrible, foggy-brained, and couldn't think after being in the office. He refused to go in for any reason, and was irritated that I continued working there. I was undeterred. Work kept me sane and I was going to continue working. Wayne set up a folding table work station near the garage's washer, dryer, and bathroom grouping. He tried to work in the kids' trailer but there wasn't enough room there. Luckily, he found the garage acceptable.

Wayne and I were very concerned about the possibility of mold contaminating the kids' trailer, so we updated our protocol for exiting a contaminated building. Only he and I could go in a contaminated building, not the kids. I followed a strict series of steps when leaving the office at the end of the day. I removed my headscarf (the newest addition to my office uniform), and left my dirty flip flops (marked by a large "D" written in white correction pen) outside the office. I grabbed a clean towel and clothes from the garage laundry, and left those on the handrail outside the kids' trailer. I yelled in the trailer door, "Cover your eyes! I'm coming in to take a shower." I undressed outside and used the trailer door to block the view from backyard neighbors, while hoping no one drove on the road in front of us. I dropped my dirty clothes on the ground outside the trailer, then walked through the trailer naked (the kids hid behind books and wished they were anywhere else, I suppose). I showered, dressed, and immediately washed my contaminated work clothes. I dunked my flip flops marked "C" for "Clean" in a Clorox solution to eliminate mold spores gathered during the two-minute trip to the travel trailer, then dried them and put them back on. I repeated this process every day.

Just when I was certain nothing else could possibly happen, Wayne climbed into the kids' trailer one morning for breakfast and discovered water running across their kitchen floor. Wayne and Justin dried the floor and under the cabinets, then tore out the carpet. Wayne discovered a small leak in the water heater and ordered a new one. I tried to be normal and remain positive, but was terribly stressed and probably dysfunctional at that point. All our buildings were either contaminated or had experienced a water leak and were possibly on track to contamination. Two days later, their trailer started smelling bad, which was incredibly depressing. I knew I couldn't take any more of this, and knew Wayne and the kids couldn't either.

Christine won an art scholarship from the Houston Livestock Show and Rodeo, so all five of us drove in for the award ceremony and evening concert. Wayne sprayed the office, bedroom, and trailer before we left for Houston.

It was life-affirming to relax and listen to music in a festive public setting that evening. During the concert, Wayne and I decided that if the kids' trailer got mold we'd move to an apartment until they finished school. The next day their trailer smelled better, so we hoped maybe it would be okay.

We took the kids to Pleasant Hills to look for houses. We enjoyed the drive, then spent several nights in a nice hotel. It wasn't luxurious, but I was ecstatic to bathe and sleep in a spotless hotel room. We teased, laughed, and settled into the undeniable happiness that arrives after enduring a severe storm. While driving through a beautiful neighborhood Friday evening,

I obsessed over scenes I imagined behind lamp-lit windows. I *knew* those families were playing fun board games around the dining table after warm baths, everyone squeaky-clean and relaxed before bed. I wanted that life for my family so badly I whispered "covet" toward the passenger window. We laughed when backseat voices softly chanted, "Covet, covet, covet!" every time I mentioned liking a house.

The third house on our Saturday tour was an unoccupied brick ranch surrounded by stately oak trees. Wayne and I were shocked as the familiar scent of mold greeted us as we entered the front door. We made eye contact, then I followed Wayne out with the kids trailing behind. We knew mold was possible in any home, but were devastated to discover it on the very first day house-hunting. Wayne lost his sense of smell and got a sore throat after walking in the moldy house, and didn't recover until the next morning. Irritated, he modified our house tour protocol so he wouldn't be put out of commission for an entire day each time we were exposed.

Wayne had gone from being the master fixer and cleaner to being the most sensitive to mold. In fact, his extensive exposure from all the cleaning and fixing he did probably led to his extreme physical reaction. Based on our experience, we expected reactions to mold to disappear within a few days of exposure. Wayne wasn't willing for either parent to be out of commission during the home tours.

Our new protocol required that Justin accompany the realtor for the initial walk-through of each house. (While we listened to the realtor's opinion, Wayne relied heavily on our family's experienced mold-detection skills.) Justin walked through, alert for musty smells and a range of physical reactions: headache, earache, sore throat, runny nose, dizziness, light-headedness, or disorientation. If Justin said the house was clean, then Christine and Shelby went inside. If they said it was fine, then I'd quickly walk through. If I didn't notice a problem, then Wayne would venture inside.

House viewing ceased when a family member said it wasn't acceptable. Wayne was so sensitive by this time that when exposed, he couldn't smell anything and sometimes couldn't concentrate until the next day. The goal of our elaborate process was to protect Wayne as much as possible. We encountered two homes with signs of mold during our first weekend, occasions when the kids cut a visit short. We didn't find a home on our first trip. Finding a mold-free home wouldn't be as easy as expected.

24

COULD HAVE DONE WITHOUT THIS

While excited to have a tentative plan to eventually move to Pleasant Hills, we still had to function in our deteriorating living conditions.

Our bedroom continued to be a huge problem, so we slept with the windows open and no air-conditioning. Julia, our wonderful house cleaner, cleaned the kids' trailer and our portable buildings every week. One week she vacuumed the bedroom floor and walls, then we mopped the entire garage floor with a bleach solution. A few days later, Wayne and I sprayed and wiped down the bedroom and the office, again. I took jackets from the office and put them in the garage laundry basket so they could be washed.

Wayne called me to come outside the office. Standing several feet away, he demanded, "Did you put jackets from the office in the garage laundry?"

I nodded slowly, surprised at how upset he was.

"You know I can't be around mold and you bring it out to me, out to the only place I have left to work? You know I can't think after I've been exposed." He paced back and forth. "Where am

I supposed to work?"

I stepped forward to say I was sorry, and he retreated. "I don't know how this is going to work. I can't do more than I'm already doing. I need a safe, clean place where I can think. And you've got to help keep it safe!"

I gulped. "I'm sorry. It won't happen again."

"It better not. You might not mind the office, but that place is poison." He called back as he turned to walk away, "Keep everything in it far away from me."

Another lesson learned (or actually re-learned)—clothing from a contaminated building had to be washed immediately.

When I checked on the kids that evening, they were sprawled comfortably on beds functioning as desks, tables, and dressers. "You guys are so adaptable!" I exclaimed.

I sat on the corner of Justin's bed while he scooted his feet up to make room for me. I was so proud of how well they'd adjusted to our circumstances. "You know that this experience made us resilient. You guys won't give up when things get tough later in life!"

Shelby looked up from her book and grinned. "When someone is mean at school, I just remember they can't really hurt me, not really. I think, 'What can they do, give me toxic mold? I already have that!'" She shrugged her shoulders. "We live in trailers, and I'm fine. They really can't do much to hurt me."

Christine said the mold improved her sense of humor, then offered an example. "One morning the fog was really bad, so my friends described how thick the fog was. Ashley said it was so thick she couldn't see the edge of her driveway, Sam said he couldn't see the edge of his house, then I said I couldn't see the edge of my travel trailer. They burst out laughing, saying they never knew I was so funny!" Our mold experience added a new level to her sense of humor.

Unfortunately, the living conditions were harsher for Wayne and me. Wayne called me out of the office again a few days later and announced, "I'm going to buy a new building where I can sleep and work."

I nodded slightly and waited.

Wayne grimaced. "No one. *No one* will be allowed in or out except me!"

I stayed silent, more than a little shocked at his change in behavior.

"I'm tired of trying to office in the garage. I'm sick of cleaning everything. I'm sick of waking up every morning, thinking, 'What in the hell do I have to clean today?'"

I was surprised by his declaration, more so when he simply turned away and walked off.

Wayne was finally wearing out. I was surprised. He had never given up before, and never denied us anything he had. He was a share-the-last-bite kind of guy, sharing even when famished or exhausted. The last bite of chocolate cake or last sip of wine was mine if I asked. I knew he wasn't acting out of selfishness, but out of self-preservation. He was more sensitive to mold and couldn't manage without a safe place to rest and work. If he needed his own refuge, I wouldn't stand in his way. We were worn down, and we both needed support.

Surprisingly, he returned to fixing things a few days later. He installed a new hot water heater in the kids' trailer while Christine and I attended a state debate competition. He delivered a trailer load of junk to the dump and took possibly salvageable items to a storage building at the farm. We'd been weeding out items for months. If an item smelled, or if we knew it couldn't be thoroughly cleaned, it was history. Wayne turned on an old computer outside in the garage, and it spewed filthy air that gave me an immediate, sharp earache. The computer had been "cleaned" by CleanHome, but obviously it wasn't clean at all. Instead, it was contaminated with other people's mold. I had never had an immediate sharp earache in my old house. That computer went to the dump.

Clinton from Community Cleaners delivered our clean clothes and we paid the $2,500 bill. We didn't want the clothes back because we didn't have a safe place to put them, but he couldn't store them longer. So we shoved plastic-draped clothes, sheets, comforters, and blankets into the utility trailer. The utility trailer smelled bad, but we had to put the items somewhere. A week later, I finally had time to remove the four smelliest boxes from the utility trailer, only to discover gray mold growing on the leather purses, shoes, and belts. Our professionally cleaned leather shoes, purses, and belts were covered with furry light-gray mold. No wonder the utility trailer smelled bad. Our cleaned clothes were no longer clean—big surprise. This was more information I learned the hard way; leather items exposed to toxic mold cannot be cleaned. Contaminated leather must be trashed.

Christine received a letter from her first choice for college, but was too nervous to open it. She asked me to drive her to church choir practice so she could open the letter in the parking lot. She said the pastor and choir would boost her up if it was bad news and she wanted to share it with them if it was good news. Christine squealed as she announced she'd be a freshman in the fall. I watched her skip toward the church clutching the letter. If we could hold on for a few more months, everything would be fine.

I felt terrible about putting the kids through this, although we consistently tried to make good decisions and couldn't have prevented much of it. I apologized to Shelby and Justin almost every day while driving them home from school.

Shelby had finally heard enough and demanded from the back seat, "Stop apologizing, Mom! One of my friends said there's mold next to his shower and some friends live in trailers. It's not going to get better for them. I know it will get better for us, so stop apologizing! We're fine!"

I was relieved by her reaction. Shelby was right; our life would get better, although I wasn't sure what else we'd experience before then. At some point our situation would get better. For other people, it might not. Our kids were resilient. *Maybe my mom was right. Just love them, do your best to care for them, and they'll be fine.* I stopped apologizing so often.

There was one remaining house in our school district that might work for us; we'd been waiting for it to go on the market. It was large enough and appeared nice on the outside. It captured my day-dreams for months. It provided hope that our kids could remain in their schools until graduation.

I was devastated during the walk-through. I'd expected a reasonably up-to-date home given the high asking price but was met with pink bathroom fixtures, an avocado-green kitchen, claustrophobically narrow halls, and walls that alternated between heavy floral wallpaper and dark wood paneling. I was glad it didn't appear to have mold, but I didn't have time or energy to renovate, especially at their asking price. Once outside, our realtor slipped on her most upbeat voice to ask what I thought. I'm sure I blindsided her when I snapped, "What do I think? I think we're moving to the Hill Country." *A bubblegum-pink toilet, come on!*

I drove back to my toxic house with my thoughts in such an intense tangled mess I may have talked aloud as I prayed,

"Please God, I know I'm a bit slow sometimes. Make it perfectly clear, clear enough even for me. Will we ever be able to live here or should we give up trying?" I heard an immediate response as I drove over the low-water crossing into our neighborhood. A clear one-sentence answer arrived in a kind, baritone voice: "You will never live here again."

Great, I was either hallucinating or conversing with God. Either way the answer was clear; we weren't staying—we'd move to the Hill Country.

COULD HAVE DONE WITHOUT
THIS AS WELL

I called our school district to see if our kids could finish school remotely; we wanted to move to a Hill Country apartment while we finished looking for a house. I asked the superintendent, "Mr. Smith, we've been fighting toxic mold for almost two years and our living conditions are horrible. Would it be okay if our kids did their schoolwork remotely? We could come back for meetings and tests, anything you want." I paused, then asked a critical question, "Christine is slated to be valedictorian, so I want to make sure this won't affect her status."

Mr. Smith didn't need to check; his answer was immediate. "Mrs. Milberger, if you move from the school district even one day before the last day of school, your daughter will lose her position as valedictorian. I'm sorry, but those are the rules."

I relayed the conversation to Wayne that night. "I can't believe they won't let us leave even a week in advance! They have no idea how bad our living conditions are!"

Wayne said, "We can't jeopardize her standing, right? She worked so hard to become valedictorian. It's her dream, right?"

"Definitely. She'd be devastated; we can't take that from her, not after all her hard work. Besides, the kids are safe; their trailer is clean. It's safe where they sleep and spend their time." I shifted to face Wayne directly. "You and I are the ones suffering in a contaminated bedroom—without air-conditioning!"

"Exactly. We just have to gut it out for a few more months until we move." Wayne leaned forward. "I can do it, can you?"

I shrugged. "It's not fun, but I can do it."

My life was a series of do-overs. Got up. Waved kids off to school. Worked. Cleaned office to remove toxic mold. Cleaned bedroom to breathe at night. Cleaned possessions. Argued with remediators. Documented phone calls. Updated lawyer. Prepared meals. Looked for new home. Tried to act normal when our lives were anything but normal. Repeat.

We set our sights on the Hill Country. All we had to do was find a house, finish school, get rid of our current house, clean or discard possessions, move, and start over. The most important, all-encompassing goal was to move without contaminating our new, yet-unfound, home.

We had a lot on our plate and we had to do it all while acting sane, and civil to our kids and each other. I called apartments for options, but they were all full. The only clean place left was the kids' trailer, where we showered, ate, and enjoyed air-conditioning.

We took several more house-hunting trips to the Hill Country. While driving down I-10 late one Friday afternoon, I pulled out my laptop to finish invoicing. After a while I noticed Wayne glancing at the laptop. A few minutes later he pulled over on the side of the interstate, got out, and leaned in over the steering wheel to ask for my laptop while cars flew past him. He turned off my laptop and shoved it in a plastic bag. He put that into another plastic bag, opened the back of the van, and placed the double-bagged laptop on our luggage. He sat behind the wheel, then announced to the windshield, "Congratulations. You just contaminated the van."

His set jaw and silence signaled he was extremely upset, which until recently was a rare occurrence. I quietly studied the AC vent inches from my knees. I didn't notice a mold odor. The van was silent for the rest of the five-hour drive, except for the dimmed radio. Wayne stared at the road and the kids stared at their books and I stared at the dashboard vents.

Of course, spewing toxic mold from a laptop cooling fan directly into a car AC unit wasn't a good idea. How many mold experiments were we going to conduct? We'd already demonstrated that mold spores shot from a VCR cooling fan would live and multiply in a window AC unit. Now I'd unintentionally replicated the experiment with a smaller fan and AC system. I hoped the outcome would be different, but clearly Wayne didn't think it would be. I might as well sign up and get paid for conducting live field experiments.

Wayne instituted additional steps to our house-hunting protocol after that. All of us showered and changed clothes as soon as we arrived at the hotel. Our realtor picked us up at the hotel and drove us to each house. We didn't get back in our van until we drove home at the end of the trip. Our realtor was used to walking in with Justin and the rest of us entering in stages determined by Wayne's mold detection flowchart. Now chauffeuring us to each house was added to his real estate duties. I found the process frustrating, but in my role as van-contaminator, I wanted to follow the procedure. Although it was difficult, it was a sound plan and would lead us to a new home. I listened to the kids' complaints, then explained our rationale. We stuck with the protocol.

Sometimes the kids balked when they were tired or unimpressed with a house. Shelby's protests rose from the backseat after leaning forward to glimpse the fifth house one Saturday, "I want to keep reading my book. I don't want to go in; send Christine instead."

I sighed, then re-explained that Dad needed several screeners first. She countered that Justin's, Christine's, and my opinion should be enough. I didn't answer, so Wayne rolled down the windows and said, "Shelby, stay in the car if you want, but you know I had Mexican food and beans at lunch."

Shelby laughed, flung open the door, and yelled, "Dad, you are so disgusting!" as she sprinted across the yard. Another house-hunting protocol saved by a dad-joke.

I called Liz to tell her I'd mailed the check for the final testing invoice. I thanked her for her help but said we'd given up trying to clean our house.

My office continued to get worse. It was obvious that mold was growing in the window AC unit. It spewed nasty air out when it was turned on. I stopped using the air-conditioning in the office and was the only one who ever walked in. If Wayne or the kids needed me, they knocked on the window behind my head. They gave up knocking on the door because I couldn't hear knocking over *Fiddler on The Roof's* "Tradition! Tradition!" blaring from my CD player. I couldn't believe how much our lives had changed. Not only did I not see my family while working in my office, I couldn't even hear them trying to get my attention.

When Justin asked to spend the weekend at his grandparents' house, I jumped at the chance to take him. Later that night I relaxed in a long, hot bath while Justin enjoyed options from Dish TV. We slept in our own rooms surrounded by clean, cool air. We soaked up love, attention, and home-cooked meals! I felt like I might stay sane if I could simply live like this. I was grateful that Wayne's parents continued to open their home to us.

Mid-April brought tornado warnings that skipped by our little trailer park. I was pretty sure my van had survived the toxic mold spewed from my laptop, but Wayne was convinced it was contaminated and refused to ride in it. I kept driving it because it was all I had. Wayne and I were very sensitive around mold or strange odors; even dust made us react. We couldn't immediately distinguish mild contamination from dust. Once we became dizzy, or forgetful, or had an immediate sharp ear pain, we knew it was mold. We did our best to avoid—or clean—all triggers. Wayne sealed my laptop in a container with a chemical to kill mold, and I hoped it would work.

A few weeks later, Justin, Shelby, and I escaped to a play in Houston. I couldn't focus on the stage because the audience captured my attention. I was mesmerized by an elderly couple chuckling and nodding their heads close to chat. *I bet they don't smell like mold!* I watched a young couple lean back in plush seats. *They're enjoying a pleasant afternoon without children.* Everyone looked comfortable and so very clean. I scanned the audience looking for clues. *Is anyone else returning to living conditions like ours, trying to sleep in a travel trailer parked in the yard or a portable building without air-conditioning?* It was virtually impossible to sleep in 88-degree weather with matching humidity. I knew we were the only ones returning to those living conditions. I was filled with absolute and utter dread on the drive home and hoped Justin and Shelby didn't notice.

PARANOIA

In early May, we settled on a breathtaking house in a gorgeous Hill Country neighborhood. With gleaming hardwood floors, abundant natural light, and plenty of room to sleep and work, it was simply perfect. The price was higher than we wanted, but we'd finally adjusted to the area's higher home values. Wayne negotiated an offer they had accepted by the time Justin and I joined him. I could finally take a deep breath. Twenty months after the big rain, our lives would change for the better!

During the final walk-though I noticed a water stain on the deep living room windowsill. Wayne and I huddled, then notified our realtor, who brought it to the home owner's attention. The husband told us it was no big deal, sometimes there was a little water seepage during a rare hard-driving rain from the west. I made a polite, nonchalant beeline for the bedroom on the opposite side of the house and pulled back the shade to find water stains on east-facing windowsills. I showed Wayne. We smiled, disengaged from the owners, grabbed our agent, and left. We told our agent we were backing out; they could keep our earnest money. While terribly disappointed to walk away from this perfect house, I knew it was the right decision. No siren's song pulled me away this time. We were moving to find grace, and grace didn't start with leaky windows, even in a stunning home with no mold odor. We were too aware after what we had been through. We knew what could happen with a second, or third, wetting. We had to keep looking.

Once home, we tried to improve our living conditions. Wayne and I cleaned our bedroom again so we could sleep and breathe at night. We decided we wouldn't buy another air-conditioner that would be contaminated in a few days. We'd have to live without air-conditioning; no small feat as summer approached.

Justin and I were gifted with another pampering weekend at Grandmother's house. The harmony evaporated when I heard Grandmother and Grandfather coughing as they ambled past my room Sunday evening. I heard Grandmother ask Grandfather if he smelled anything in the hallway, but his answer was lost to her extensive hacking cough. She recovered and added she might postpone her heart surgery until she felt better. My body stiffened with fear; I was petrified that somehow I'd brought mold to them. I lay awake, frozen, all night. I wondered if she'd cancel her heart surgery. What if she died because I'd brought mold to their house? I fought to overcome my fear and regain rational thought. I knew I didn't bring mold. I'd been so careful. Even though it might feel like every building we used became contaminated, that wasn't the case. The bed and breakfast stayed clean, as did the kids' trailer, and our garage.

I must have looked dreadful because Grandmother's kitchen-table greeting was "You look worried." I immediately dissolved into tears and admitted I was worried. I confessed I was worried about their health; that I might have brought mold to their house. I was grateful that she dismissed my concern. She said their house was fine, she'd been sick for a while, and I was under too much stress. I took Justin to school, purchased several HEPA air purifiers, then drove fifty miles back to their house. Grandmother and Grandfather's excitement over the air purifiers lifted my mood and stalled my tears until I began driving home. Crying while driving was my new super-efficient existence.

My office attire deteriorated along with the air quality. I slipped on clunky black plastic sandals marked with a white "D," a constant reminder that they were dirty. I covered my T-shirt and shorts with Wayne's old plaid short-sleeve shirt and shoved my hair into a shower cap each time I entered the office. My concerns that the head scarf wasn't adequate protection made me decide to upgrade to clear plastic. Topped by my haggard, distracted expression, it would be easy to gain mental ward access; I'd be ushered in after one glance. I was a sight and felt worse than I looked.

Fiddler on the Roof kept me company while I worked. I lowered the volume for phone calls, then blasted it back after hanging up. I frequently worked nights since work was the only thing that made a difference. I couldn't fix our living situation but I could make progress on my mountain of work. Although it was stressful, I found the workload ideal because it kept me occupied—our reality was too painful.

With so many events screaming for my attention, I didn't notice our rescue calico kitten was no longer a kitten until she produced three gorgeous babies. I'd been too busy to notice, much less address, Patches' impending puberty. She settled her fluffy offspring in the tall canvas laundry hamper next to the garage restroom. The hamper ignited with tiny mewing sounds from roused wiggling babies every time Patches escaped for a break. Enthralled, our family spent hours cooing over the laundry hamper's soft contents. The kids begged to keep them, and we agreed. Shelby was right; cats often don't adjust to moving. Patches would probably stay to care for her babies, but we couldn't be sure about the other three cats.

The office began smelling so bad that even I had a hard time walking in. But work had eclipsed exercise as my primary sanity-saving tool and I was desperate to escape. The fact that I had plenty of work also helped. I kept the windows cracked open for fresh air while I worked.

I spent May 9—Mother's Day—cleaning our bedroom, vacuuming, mopping, and doing laundry. I guess Justin felt sorry for me, because he vacuumed the van, which, looking back, was really sweet of him.

Our bedroom was awful. It was very hard to breathe in there, but we had no place else to sleep. We opened the windows during the day so we could run the AC at night. In the mornings I woke to yellow gunky lashes glued shut over bloodshot eyes. Wayne left each morning by 5 a.m. because he couldn't stand it any longer. Oh, and his truck smelled bad, and even I had to agree that my van smelled like mold. Never, never, would I have imagined it could have become this bad.

Christine announced she had a date for the prom and needed a dress. Christine was petite, so I knew alterations would be necessary. When I factored that in along with her busy schedule, I realized she needed to buy a dress on Sunday. Shelby joined as we visited a series of Houston department stores, boutiques, and bridal shops. Christine initially occupied the dressing stall alone, only appearing when fully zipped. After several hours, she was exhausted, hungry, and ready to quit. Shelby and I crammed into her dressing room to create a two-man protocol of zipping, unzipping, and rehanging discarded gowns with a steady stream of compliments and encouragement. Christine finally stood motionless until a dress appeared on the floor in front of her, then managed to step forward and wait while we zipped her up. Finally she was too tired to step into an unzipped dress. Shelby compelled her sister forward by declaring in her best Irish accent, "Jump, Lassy, jump!" imitating Scarlett O'Hara's father from *Gone With the Wind*.

Christine chose a beautiful black dress with multiple petticoats; hemming would take forever. The dress was so full I couldn't mark the hem in the trailer because no matter where she stood, the dress touched a cabinet, bed, or wall; usually all three. Luckily our next-door neighbor allowed me to mark the dress in her living room. After several afternoons I gave up marking each layer to simply cut each to the appropriate length. Thank goodness it wasn't noticeable with all those petticoats.

Christine was beautiful in her prom dress and her date handsome in his tux. They posed for pictures on the steps of the travel trailer, then moved to the front of the house for a traditional photo shoot. The setting was stunning with lush green grass at their feet, bright white periwinkles lining the flowerbed, and alternating pink, violet, and white azaleas in full bloom. The shiny leaves and enormous white blooms of the magnolia tree stood out against the gray river rock façade.

It was surreal. After all this, the house looked perfectly normal outside, like any suburban home.

Thank God I was relatively resilient. What if I had a tendency towards drug or alcohol abuse? Actually, our life might have caused an alcoholic or drug addict to sober up; otherwise they'd never escape from the mold.

I wasn't actually that resilient. I wept every time I was alone in the car. Hunched forward, clutching the steering wheel, my thoughts pulled me in as the car sped away under my absent-minded guidance. I ignored my body's distress signals until I noticed cool tears evaporate from my cheeks. My overworked brain struggled with this new data, wondering what caused unintentional tears. Once this question was posed, the tears fell freely among the facts of our hopeless situation.

I was terrified we'd never escape from mold. I was terrified of losing my ability to think. I was terrified it could reduce me to a human slug that slumbered and drooled through life. I was terrified of not getting enough air to breathe at night. I was terrified by how easily mold spread. I worried about the effect on our kids, and wondered if they felt safe. I wondered if moving would be enough to escape this horror. I prayed that no one else would ever experience what we were going through.

After returning home, I turned off the ignition, wiped my eyes in the rearview mirror, then took a long, deep breath. Sneak-attack tears were an unsettling reminder that the stress was too much to handle, that my ignored body was sending increasingly louder cries for help to capture my attention. But we had a viable plan. I needed to hold it together for a few more months until we could escape to the Hill Country and a mold-free home.

I would keep plowing forward, working and taking care of our family, and soon the days would turn into months and we'd leave. We would start over, and not bring anything that could threaten our new, clean home. We had a plan. We just had to hang on for another month or so. Soon our lives would get back to normal.

I took a deep breath, then rechecked my eyes to ensure the crying signs weren't obvious. It was pure instinct, as fundamental as breathing, to protect Wayne and the kids from my tears, from any signs of pain. Each of us had enough on our plates.

It was a reflex reaction to shield them from additional burdens.

27

ALMOST HOME

We continued our Texas Hill Country house-hunting trips. Only a few homes were available that were large enough but not enormous. We wanted four bedrooms and an office. I wanted a bedroom for Christine's home visits so she didn't feel displaced. I wanted our kids to have privacy. We'd had enough togetherness for a while.

By mid-May we were close to making an offer on a clean, beautiful home. It was bigger than we needed, but I liked it and Wayne loved it. He was thrilled with the steel-frame construction topped by a strong metal roof—we could tear the house back to the steel frame and rebuild if needed. We didn't expect to have mold again and prayed our contingencies wouldn't be necessary. However, we discussed contingency plans often. We were so used to mold contamination that planning for it became natural. Knowing it was unlikely we'd survive another mold contamination emotionally or physically, we did everything possible to prevent it. However, it was impossible for Wayne and me not to discuss strategies for handling contamination.

The terrific news was we were close to the end. School was

out. We clapped after Christine's uplifting valedictorian speech, and cheered for the graduating class. Then we returned to doing what needed to be done—cleaning and throwing stuff away. We kept our heads down and kept on plowing, and the days turned into weeks.

But our little trailer park was miserably hot and humid. The air spewing from the AC unit was unbearable, so we left the windows cracked open for fresh air. One night I woke at 1:30 a.m. because I couldn't breathe. My eyes ached and I felt sand scrape under my eyelids. I reached up and found my eyelashes caked shut. I turned off the AC, opened the windows, then examined my bloodshot eyes in the mirror. I washed until my eyelashes were free of the milky-yellow crust, but my eyes remained inflamed. I lay in the damp sticky bed for hours, hoping to fall back to sleep so I could function when morning arrived. We'd returned to the beginning—our air wasn't safe to sleep.

I spent my days sorting and throwing away everything we couldn't clean. The family was under strict orders; if an item was porous, it must be thrown away. We couldn't bring paper of any kind: no files, notebooks, or books would go to our new house. Wayne would store important files in a storage container at the farm and the rest would be thrown away. We couldn't bring leather of any kind. No furniture would go with us, except the iron patio set. Basically, if we couldn't wash it or wipe it down, we couldn't bring it. Obviously, electronics with fans, including computers, were not allowed. We transferred important files to a thumb drive. I would get a new computer from work and Wayne would buy one, plus we'd buy one for Christine as well. It was difficult to spend so much money to start over. We'd spent like crazy over the past months, but now it felt like we were hemorrhaging money, and it would get worse after we moved.

We had no choice at this point. We could only bring what was cleanable, and everything else had to be purchased. We cleaned and packed dishes, pots and pans, utensils, linens, clothing, and the patio set. Toxic mold contamination stopped here.

We knew it was possible that a rogue toxic mold spore could stow away on some item and appear in our new house. However, we hoped that with no leaks and a dry climate it wouldn't have a place to grow.

I traded my contaminated laptop in for a clean one at work. The information technology department knew I was trading in a laptop contaminated with toxic mold. I met the IT guy outside to give him my plastic-wrapped laptop and reminded him not to turn it on inside. I had an upbeat meeting with my boss, then headed home to pick up Justin. We spent a squeaky-clean night at Grandmother's. I faxed an update to our lawyer, then collapsed into bed. We planned to get up early, pick up two cats and three kittens, drive to Pleasant Hills, and attend the closing that afternoon. We'd sleep in our new home that night.

The stress caught up with me because I woke with a searing migraine. Looking back, I find it amazing that I didn't have a migraine during the entire mold experience, not until the day we moved. I flipped on the bathroom exhaust fan for white noise while I threw up, but Grandmother heard enough to provide a hallway comment "…those headaches must really be bad." I drove for an hour with one eye open and one closed, wishing Justin was old enough to drive. Finally, my headache eased enough to open both eyes at the same time.

I parked in front of our garage for the last time. We loaded Meow Meow and Sassy and her kittens into carriers in the van. I glanced back at our house, still deceptively attractive except for the cluster of portable buildings and trailers. After a deep breath,

I pulled away from our difficult chapter, driving normally, but imagining throwing gravel as we rocketed toward our new life.

After the drive, we attended the closing and received the house keys. We purchased four twin mattresses and metal bedframes before the furniture store closed for the evening. We slid plastic-wrapped mattresses in the truck bed, then plopped them on the floor in our bedrooms.

We slept in clean air that night.

I was grateful we were finally safe.

RECOVERY

I woke after a long, deep sleep, then leisurely stretched over the edge of my mattress. I surveyed the empty room and smiled.

I operated for months in a dream-like state. While busy—there was so much still to do—I floated through my list knowing I'd rest and recharge at night. I didn't have to clean and paint to secure a few nights' sleep. I didn't worry about contamination or cleaning or breathing. Our high-stakes life was over.

I inhaled deeply and frequently in any room I chose.

We ripped up the carpet and mopped the concrete. We ate on our trusty patio table. We set up offices with camp chairs and I resumed working. The kids caught up with friends as they enjoyed summer camp. I joined a new neighbor for daily morning workouts. Our cats and fluffy kittens adjusted beautifully. Wayne moved the contaminated utility trailer to our yard so we could fax important papers—including the contents of my spiral notebook—to our new house. (We stripped by the back door and showered after finishing each day.)

I sported a goofy grin for months. Everything was easier. My shoulders dropped away from my earlobes. I never cried. I giggled for no reason. Wayne began singing as he walked down the hallway. It was reassuring to hear him singing his favorite, Bobby McFerrin's "Don't Worry, Be Happy," just like the old days.

Shelby and Justin started high school and middle school, and Christine started college in Houston. Justin immediately found a friend group and even brought a friend home after the first day of school. They walked in the back door as his friend's voice reverberated through our empty rooms, "Wow! You know how people always say they don't have any furniture, but they really do? You guys DON'T HAVE ANY FURNITURE AT ALL!"

It took time for Shelby to adjust to high school. We found a new therapist and Shelby, Wayne, and I began therapy again—Justin declined. There was a lot to unpack from our experience, and therapy helped us adjust.

We found new doctors and got checkups. I told the kids' pediatrician and my physician about our mold exposure, but didn't receive additional testing or treatment. Our children seemed fine, so we didn't pursue it further. I tried addressing my fatigue with a naturopathic mix of nutrition, supplements, and massage, then began taking thyroid medication.

Wayne tallied the value of our land, driveway, water well, and house slab to create a price for our contaminated home. He didn't assign value to the structure since he believed it should be torn down and rebuilt. A neighbor's relative asked for a tour, then said the house smelled fine. Wayne gave them copies of the final mold test reports—one reporting the house had mold and one reporting it did not—and said the house should be torn down. We received and accepted their offer but didn't stay in touch.

Wayne moved the trailers, portable buildings, and our office furniture to the farm for storage. A year later, he hired a Houston company to cover the buildings and his truck with a huge tarp, then fumigate everything with methyl bromide. Wayne thought the treatment helped, but we never brought those possessions to our new home. I traded the van for a clean-smelling used replacement.

The remediators dropped their lawsuit demanding payment for cleaning and storage, and we stopped paying a lawyer. Our belongings remained locked in the Houston warehouse, then disappeared. We later heard the remediators auctioned off all of our possessions.

We began socializing, but Wayne and I had a difficult time controlling our story-telling after our experience. We could participate in polite conversation until someone asked what brought us to the area. It was tough to transition to other topics after mentioning "toxic mold." We sometimes couldn't stop talking until shocked companions looked for an exit. We finally started saying we moved because of the beautiful weather.

Wayne and I remained very sensitive to odors—chemicals, mold, urine, dust, mildew, perfume, and others—and Wayne was bothered more than me. Unfortunately, our bedroom closet smelled like urine; apparently this was a preferred spot for the previous owners' cats. We noticed the odor during our walk-through visits, but thought mopping would be enough. It wasn't. This began a rather unpleasant time: our "please smell this" phase. After several cleanings, Wayne began removing baseboards. Each time he removed one, he asked me to smell the baseboard, then smell the closet to see if it was clean. He still wasn't satisfied after several repetitions, so he removed the bottom of the built-in shoe rack. I tried to be understanding when he asked me to sniff along the floor, but found this request upsetting. I didn't want to crouch on the floor and inhale—I had traumatic memories of the last time Wayne asked me to smell baseboards. After removing the entire shoe rack, Wayne finally deemed the closet clean and released me from smelling duty.

One dramatic moment jolted me from my dream-like state. Floor tile installation began well as installers worked in our bedroom while Wayne removed the hallway baseboards. When he removed one baseboard it yanked a nail from the water pipe behind it. Water flowed across the concrete floor. Wayne yelled for me to grab a mop as he ran outside to shut off the water.

A worker rushed to help, then announced, "You know, you need to clean that up right away because it can cause mold."

"Yes, I know about mold," I responded curtly, unwilling to share what I knew about leaks and mold.

I struggled to control my fear—the consequences of a similar leak had been disastrous—as I swung the mop in a wide arc. *Not all leaks cause mold.*

I drug the mop back. *Not all mold is toxic.*

I swung it right. *Many homes are remediated.*

I pulled the mop left. *Our mold was an extreme case.*

It took a while for us to buy a dining table, coffee tables, chairs, and couches. We were frightened of used furniture after our experience, so antiques were no longer an option. I added books and knickknacks, artwork, and area rugs until the house looked comfortable. I added lamps after I finally noticed lamplight makes houses look inviting at night.

After a few years of relative bliss, Wayne asked for my opinion about property on a hill overlooking Pleasant Hills.

His eyes lit up as he described the location, "It would be a great place for a winery."

I wasn't surprised. Wayne frequently talked about building a winery and had done lots of research. I smiled as I watched him gush about winemaking. *After all he'd been through, Wayne should do whatever makes him happy.* It was a bit naïve—building and operating a winery is a huge undertaking—but it was time for a new chapter.

29

SURVIVOR

For the first decade after moving, my reaction to mold was swift and strong. Whether I saw a water stain in a coffee shop or fuzzy mold in a café restroom, I froze like a deer caught in headlights, then remained immobile as my body wrestled with modified versions of the fight or flight response. A full-speed run was inappropriate, so I settled for a purse-clutching center-aisle stroll for the door. As far as the fight response, I knew I couldn't fight mold and didn't carry Clorox Clean-Up with me. I would back away with my chin ducked to my chest, as if pretending to be invisible would deter spores from infecting my hair and clothes.

Twenty years after moving, I'm no longer preoccupied with mold—but there are lingering effects. Traveling is particularly difficult because of our heightened sensitivity. I pore over Tripadvisor hotel reviews and shun locations with mentions of mildew or musty odors.

We faithfully avoid moisture and humidity in the house. Towels are hung up, shower doors propped open, and refrigerator bins rotated. The washing machine doesn't run without an adult present, but we've eased into using the dishwasher's "delay start" mode. To avoid frozen pipes, Wayne drains the house water lines before we leave for a trip during cold weather. The damp mop always basks in the wonderful Texas sun until fully dry. Our lives have returned to a semblance of normalcy in that mold and mold-avoidance are no longer the focus of everyday life.

But twenty years after leaving our contaminated home, it's still difficult to get help with symptoms of toxic mold exposure. Two years ago, my concerns over lingering health issues (fatigue, frequent urination, and excessive sweating) were dismissed by my primary care physician. I sought help from a naturopathic physician after hearing toxic mold survivors complain about frequent urination as the body attempts to flush out toxins. A mycotoxin urine test revealed high levels of Ochratoxin A, a mycotoxin that flourishes in damp/flooded buildings. Shocked to find mold living inside me—especially one tied to kidney damage and cancer—I began a detoxing program including targeted supplements, binders, teas, saunas, and a healthier diet. Instead of reducing my symptoms, I became more exhausted after several months. I stayed on the detox program because I'd been warned that detoxing was a long, complicated process and I'd feel worse before I felt better. I finally improved some after following the expensive, time-consuming protocol—plus a few coffee enemas and intravenous oxygen therapy treatments—for eight more months. I lost faith after my annual mycotoxin urine test revealed an even higher level of Ochratoxin A, as well as high levels of Citrinin (multiple mold species). My nutritionist said mold results can increase and more mold types can appear during detoxing, so I needed to stay on the protocol. I gave up because I was frustrated with the lack of data supporting the detox process. I stopped paying for supplements, IVs, and appointments that weren't covered by my insurance for a process that didn't appear effective.

I'm grateful we survived with minimal damage—at least that's how it appears. Our children grew up, graduated from college, and have wonderful jobs. All of us, including our grandchildren, appear relatively healthy. I now believe Mom's advice that loving and caring for our children is enough.

EPILOGUE

I know life can change in an instant, and it can take years to recover from a disaster.

Our experience left me grateful for simple things like the morning's first cup of coffee, time spent with friends and family, and clean air. Our experience also made me more anxious about mold and leaks. We aren't the only ones who had a difficult time remediating their home or recovering from toxic mold exposure. Tens of thousands of people belong to toxic mold survivor Facebook groups.

I met a local couple who had an experience similar to ours a few years ago. I saw an article in the paper about a couple who burned their home and possessions after fighting toxic mold for eighteen months. I showed Wayne the photo of the parents and two gorgeous children. We couldn't attend their fundraiser but sent a card and donation. Wayne insisted the card's message say they were wise to burn their house, and we should have burned ours. The couple, Mark and Kate, sent us a thank you card and we arranged to meet weeks later at our winery tasting room.

Mark was tall and lanky with a thick brown beard, while Kate and the children had porcelain skin, large clear eyes, and glossy dark hair. The children drew and colored while the adults talked. Within minutes, we found our experiences so similar and our connection so strong that we laughed and finished each other's sentences. We relayed stressful stories about not knowing how to fix our homes or adequately clean items. We talked about the feeling of utter defeat after months of being ill, cleaning, and failing. We shared stories of family and friends not understanding or even dismissing our experience.

Kate smiled shyly. "Mark cried when he read Wayne's note saying it was the right decision to burn our house. He was touched that someone who understood mold said burning the house was the correct thing to do. Mark's father was unsupportive, insisting he was crazy to burn the house and our possessions."

"Crazy, well, we can show you crazy." Mark grinned. "Kate's first reaction to mold is her forehead becomes inflamed and bright red, then she gets a fever. After a while she becomes too weak to even function or eat, and she finally crawls into a ball and doesn't move. It's frightening to see her like that, and I can't stand it." Kate reached over to squeeze Mark's hand.

Mark's voice grew louder. "After that happened several times, I started jumping into action. If I walked in the house and noticed her forehead was red and puffy, or even pink, I immediately scanned the room to see if there was anything new in the house."

Mark jumped up, then paced in front of the tasting room fireplace. "I kept looking for something new, something I hadn't seen before. Maybe I'd spot a gift, like a stuffed bear on the coffee table. Since *my* first reaction to mold is a tingling around my mouth, I'd grab the bear and rub it up and down my beard, then wait." Mark lifted the imaginary bear and deliberately rubbed it along his chin from ear to ear.

Mark dropped the imaginary bear to his side. "Then I demanded to know from whoever was there—friends, parents, neighbors, whoever was in the house—I *insisted* they tell me if the item was new, and what store it came from. They were usually stunned, so while they struggled to answer, I checked to see if my face was tingling yet."

Mark stopped pacing, tilted his face toward the ceiling, and absentmindedly caressed his beard.

I watched, transfixed, as Mark stared into space.

Mark returned his focus to us. "If my face tingled, that was it! I grabbed each new item, even if it was a gift just delivered, and marched across the living room. I opened the front door and flung the gift as far as I could. Every time I threw something, I shouted the name of the store where I thought it came from." As Mark violently hurled pretend gifts through the imaginary open door, he mimicked in a hushed bark, "'H Mart, huh? Well, that's gone. Classy Consignments? Well, that's out of here!' Then I stomped around the room searching for more new items."

Mark plopped down on his chair and grinned as I rocked back and forth in laughter. I knew that feeling, I had lived that feeling. This is what my friends saw as I excused myself to wait on the sidewalk while they shopped. I had finally found my people.

Mold survivors are a little bit crazy and a little bit paranoid about mold.

Given what we've gone through, that makes us very sane.

AFTERWORD

I can't offer advice about mold, mold remediation, or mold detoxing. I only know what worked—and what didn't work—for us.

I wrote this book for several reasons.

I wanted to write about our experience for the toxic mold sufferers who are struggling to recover—physically, mentally, emotionally, and financially. Even with our resources, it took about eight years to feel like I'd recovered enough to consider writing about our experience, then additional years to find the time, gain writing skills, and begin. I wrote MOLDed for the toxic mold victims who don't have the time or energy to tell their stories.

I wanted to remind people to be grateful for everyday life because it can change overnight. I wanted to remind people to be grateful for simple things, like clean air to breathe at night.

I wanted to write an exciting true story so more people would understand how hard it is to recover from toxic mold, and the symptoms toxic mold exposure can cause.

I wanted people to know that even in 2024, it is still very difficult to get help with symptoms of toxic mold exposure.

I wrote MOLD*ed* because we need better tools to deal with toxic mold. More people will suffer from toxic mold exposure as climate change brings more extreme storms across the United States. We need more research on toxic mold's effects and how to detox from exposure. This research should be made available and taught in traditional medical schools. The CDC website needs to provide information on the mental, physical, and emotional impacts of toxic mold exposure, and stop dismissing victims as immune-compromised individuals suffering from allergies. We need to ensure that disreputable remediators can't hide poor reviews or lawsuits from potential customers. Homeowners need to know if their home, in their climate, with their molds, can be remediated. Homeowners shouldn't spend almost two years and countless dollars trying to fix what, in some cases, is unfixable.

Life can change in a second. There are solutions, help, and treatments for cancer, depression, or home loss due to hurricane or fire. I want mold victims to be helped instead of being ignored and left to figure out their own solutions.

My updated mantra is:

Not all leaks cause mold.
Not all mold is toxic.
Many homes are remediated.
But when it is toxic mold,
victims need help and quality information.

THANK YOU

Thanks to my husband, Wayne, for tolerating my determination to revisit our horrific experience. Kudos for rarely responding to my questions or updates with "I don't want to talk about toxic mold anymore! I lived through it once and that was more than enough for me."

Thanks to my mom for listening. I didn't truly understand the power of listening—your ability to provide hope from thousands of miles away—until I felt hope swell in my chest after a phone conversation. Knowing you cared about what we were going through made a huge difference.

Thanks to my mother-in-law (and father-in-law—a prince among men) for hosting my son and me. You didn't worry about stray mold spores as you welcomed us to your home's clean luxury. Those visits helped keep me sane.

Thanks to my kids for demonstrating resilience and hope in its purest form. You knew we'd take care of you even when we were unsure.

Thanks to the Birds writing group, possibly the kindest, funniest, wisest band of Zooming writers I could hope to write, critique, and goal-set with. Anna, Carole, Karen, Teri, and Vanessa—it's an honor to regularly share Zoom squares with you. I hope we write together until the very end.

Thanks to my in-person writing group—especially Larry and Ron—for keeping the lights on for small-town writers.

Thanks to Jackie, Danette, Jeanne, and Beth for providing thoughtful feedback on the manuscript. Your input was extremely valuable.

Thanks to Brooks Becker, the best proofreader I could have hoped for. While humbling to see how much I needed your skilled eye, I appreciate every red mark.

Thanks to Vanessa Mendozzi for typesetting and the perfect cover design. I never knew I wanted typesetting until I saw what you offered.

Thanks to the Writers' League of Texas for providing incredible writing classes. Some of my favorite instructors and editors include Diane Zinna, Ron Sebold, Jessica Wilbanks, and Deanna Roy. I was so impressed with Diane Zinna, I became a permanent morning circle member and then joined her for the best-ever Book in a Year class.

Thanks to the Moldies who've bravely forged a path back to a clean home and good health, then reach back to help others do the same.

I hope this book inspires discussion and research, and leads to more quality information about mold, mold illnesses and treatment, and mold remediation.

ABOUT THE AUTHOR

CAROL MILBERGER is a retired psychologist and management consultant, former winery owner, mother, and grandmother who began writing to relay her experience with toxic mold. Her essays have appeared in *The New York Times*, *Wired*, *Next Avenue*, *Insider*, and elsewhere. Carol lives with her husband in the Texas Hill Country. Find out more at **carolmilberger.com**.

Dear Reader,

Thank you for choosing *MOLDed: A Memoir of Loss & Resilience*. Toxic mold contamination is rarely covered extensively from the homeowners' perspective.

Your review on Amazon will help other readers discover the book and contribute to the growing conversation about this important topic. Please consider sharing your thoughts to let others know how this book impacted you!

With gratitude,
Carol Milberger